SPITFIRE
THE CANADIANS

*S/L Wally McLeod, 443 Squadron, 1944.
McLeod was the pilot of 21-E (MK 636) on D-Day
and the official top RCAF ace. His aircraft
is pictured on the front cover.*
– Thelma McLeod

High Flight

Oh! I have slipped the surly bonds of earth
    And danced the skies on laughter-silvered wings;
Sunward I've climbed, and joined the tumbling mirth
    Of sun-split clouds—and done a hundred things
You have not dreamed of—wheeled and soared and swung
    High in the sunlit silence. Hov'ring there
I've chased the shouting wind along, and flung
    My eager craft through footless halls of air.

Up, up the long, delirious, burning blue
    I've topped the windswept heights with easy grace
Where never lark, nor even eagle flew—
    And, while with silent lifting mind I've trod
The high untrespassed sanctity of space
    Put out my hand and touched the face of God.

JOHN GILLESPIE MAGEE JR.
412 Squadron, RCAF

SPITFIRE
THE CANADIANS

ROBERT BRACKEN

Foreword by A.V.M. J.E. "Johnnie" Johnson
Artwork by Ron Lowry

(Stoddart)

BOSTON MILLS PRESS

Canadian Cataloguing in Publication Data

Bracken, Robert, 1950-
Spitfire: the Canadians

ISBN 1-55046-148-6

1. Spitfire (Fighter planes).
2. World War, 1939-1945 - Aerial operations, Canadian.
3. World War, 1939-1945 - Personal narratives, Canadian.
I. Title.

D792.C2B73 1995   940.54'4971   C95-931054-1

© 1995 Robert Bracken
Design and typography by Daniel Crack
Kinetics Design & Illustration
Printed in Canada

First published in 1995 by
The Boston Mills Press
132 Main Street
Erin, Ontario
N0B 1T0
519-833-2407 fax 833-2195

An affiliate of
Stoddart Publishing Co. Limited
34 Lesmill Road
North York, Ontario
M3B 2T6

The publisher gratefully acknowledges the support of the Canada Council, Ontario Arts Council and Ontario Publishing Centre in the development of writing and publishing in Canada.

> Stoddart Books are available for bulk purchase for sales promotions, premiums, fundraising and seminars. For details, contact:
>
> Special Sales Department
> Stoddart Publishing Co. Limited
> 34 Lesmill Road
> North York, Ontario M3B 2T6
> Tel. 1-416-445-3333
> Fax 1-416-445-5967

Preceding page: The Spitfire IXs of 411 Grizzly Bear Squadron at Heesch, the Netherlands, March 22, 1945. – PAC 115095

Contents

Foreword by A.V.M. J.E. "Johnnie" Johnson	7
Preface	9
The Battle of Britain *Keith "Skeets" Ogilvie,* 609 Sqn.	11
The Battle of Britain *Jan Zurakowski,* 234, 609 Sqns.	13
The Battle of Britain *J.S. "Stew" Young,* 234 Sqn.	15
R.S. Tuck's Last Flight *Al Harley,* 401 Sqn.	16
The Search for Paddy Finucane *Bob Morrow,* 402 Sqn.	21
Flying the Mark V Spitfire *Ron McGarva,* 421 Sqn.	23
Letters Home *Norm Bretz,* 401, 402, 411, 416 Sqns.	24
The Dieppe Raid *Don R. Morrison,* 401 Sqn.	26
Dieppe *George Aitken,* 403 Sqn.	31
City of Oshawa Squadron *R.H. "Kelly" Walker,* 416 Sqn.	35
Flying the Mark V Spitfire *C.M. "Chuck" Steele,* 411 Sqn.	39
Malta *Noel "Buzz" Ogilvie,* 130, 185, 401, 403 Sqns.	40
A Woman in a Spitfire *Marion Orr,* ATA, Ferry Command	42
The Skychief II *Richard "Hap" Beall,* 421 Sqn.	45
Ramrod 133: My First Mission *Len Thorne,* 421 Sqn.	47
Ramrod to Montdidier *Norm Chevers,* 403 Sqn.	49
My System *George "Buzz" Beurling,* 403, 412 Sqns.	51
We Bagged a 109 a Minute *Lloyd Chadburn,* 402, 416 Sqns.	53
Rhubarb Over Holland *Art Sager,* 416, 443 Sqns.	57
A Belly Landing *Sten Lundberg,* 416 Sqn.	59
Dogfight Over Italy *Bert Houle,* 145, 213, 417 Sqns.	61
Dogfight Over Anzio *J.J. Doyle,* 417 Sqn.	63
Shot Down! *Ralph Nickerson,* 421 Sqn.	64
Reconnaissance *M.G. "Mac" Brown,* 400 Sqn.	69
Fighter Reconnaissance *Ken Lawson,* 414 Sqn.	71
Recon Over Germany *Warren Middleton,* 430 Sqn.	73
Spitfire Pilots in Hotspur Gliders *Thomas Koch,* 401 Sqn.	75
D-Day and Normandy *Larry Seath,* 400 Sqn.	77
D-Day *George Lawson,* 402 Sqn.	78
D-Day *W.A. "Art" Bishop,* 401 Sqn.	79

Aircraft Paintings *Ron Lowry*	81
D-Day, D-Day, D-Day *Cecil Brown,* 403 Sqn.	97
Ground Crew *Bill Reale,* 441, 402 Sqns.	101
"Johnnie" Johnson's Thirty-third Victory *Guy Mott,* 441 Sqn.	103
"Johnnie" Johnson *Bill Weeks,* 442 Sqn.	104
"A Short While Into the Sun" *Bill Weeks,* 442 Sqn.	105
Close Combat *I.F. "Hap" Kennedy,* 401 Sqn.	107
Down in a Minefield *Stu Tosh,* 403 Sqn.	109
Three in One Mission *Wilf Banks,* 412 Sqn.	111
Shooting Down a V-1 Flying Bomb *Bill Austin,* 402 Sqn.	113
R & R the Hard Way *Les Foster,* 443 Sqn.	114
Nijmegen *"Kelly" Walker,* 441 Sqn.	116
How I Shot Down a 109 *Sid Bregman,* 441 Sqn.	118
The Jet Job *J.J. Boyle,* 411 Sqn.	119
Christmas Eve, 1944 *John Patus,* 416 Sqn.	121
Recollections *G.D. Cameron,* 401, 402 Sqns.	122
Living on the Edge *Cecil Mann,* Ground Crew, 401 Sqn.	124
Outfoxed *J.J. Boyle,* 411 Sqn.	127
Recollections *Chuck Darrow,* 416 Sqn.	129
"Johnnie" Johnson's Beer *Brian "Blackie" MacConnell,* 402 Sqn.	130
Shooting Down a Jet Bomber *Brian "Blackie" MacConnell,* 402 Sqn.	131
Dive-bombing *Bill Harper,* 421 Sqn.	133
Ground Attack *Lloyd Burford,* 421 Sqn.	135
The Lost Legion: Canadians in the RAF *Paul Ostrander,* 155 Sqn. RAF, Burma	139
The Last Day: Flying the Mark XIV Spitfire *Jack Rigby,* 402 Sqn.	141
Spitfires at Rockcliffe *Tom Percival and C.W. "Chuck" Doodson,* Rockcliffe	143
The Occupation of Germany *Walter Thompson,* 416 Sqn.	145
Spitfires in Israel *Denny Wilson,* 101 Sqn. IDF	148
Flying the Last Spitfires *Guy Mott,* Weapons Officer, 441, 18, 80 Sqns.	150
Acknowledgments	152
Canadian Fighter Pilots	154
Aircraft Drawings *Ralph Clint*	156

FOREWORD

Air Vice-Marshal J.E. "Johnnie" Johnson
C.B., C.B.E., D.S.O., D.F.C., D.L.

DURING the Second World War, I knew several Canadian fighter pilots, but my real association with the Canadians began in the early spring of 1943 when I was appointed wing commander flying of the Kenley Wing (403 and 416 Squadrons) and ended some two years later in the spring of 1945 when I left 127 Wing at Petit Brogel, Belgium, shortly before the Rhine crossing and a few weeks before the end of the war in Germany. We were fortunate in flying the elegant Spitfire IX, whose only disadvantage was its lack of range, but which, as a defensive fighter, had no equal.

During these two years we saw a fair amount of action, and I think the highlight of 1943 was escorting the B-17s of the Eighth USAAF (the Mighty Eighth) as they fought their way deep into Germany and proved their success in daylight bombing. Before the arrival of the long-range Mustang—the most significant fighter of the Second World War—the Americans took some hard knocks. But they pressed on and eventually won a great victory, wresting from the enemy the command of the daylight skies over Europe and exposing the heart of Germany to bombing.

In the spring of 1944 I became wing commander flying of a new Canadian Spitfire wing (144), and on June 15, 1944, we were the first Spitfire outfit to move into Normandy, at Saint-Croix-sur-Mer. From the beachhead our fighter-bombers stunned and paralyzed the German armies, which found their own blitzkrieg tactics now turned against them.

When 144 Wing was disbanded I went to 127 Wing of the RCAF, at Crépon. We soon began the long trek across northwest Europe, only to be halted by the Rhine, Montgomery's failure at Arnhem, and the onset of winter. By the following spring it was all over.

W/C "Johnnie" Johnson in his Spitfire IX, JE-J (MK 392). – Len Thorne

Spitfire: The Canadians is a collection of the stories of Canadian Second World War fighter pilots. Such men lived a strange life that alternated between short periods of intense urgency in the air and long spells of uneventful tedium on the ground. Once in the air, every pilot became an integral part of his Spitfire. Every pilot's dedication was well concealed beneath an outward gaiety.

F/O Brian "Blackie" MacConnell, 402 Squadron, flew this Spitfire XIV, AE-J (RN 119) on April 19, 1945, when he shot down a German Ar 234B jet. Heesch, the Netherlands, March 4, 1945. – DND PL 42434

Spitfires from 411 Squadron warming up in Heesch, the Netherlands, March 22, 1945. In the foreground is DB-P (MJ 334). – PA 115094

PREFACE

EARLY in my research for this book, I was asked what could possibly be added to the Spitfire story after all this time. Since I had already interviewed a number of veterans who had flown or serviced the Spitfire, I was able to reply that much remained untold. Canada's enormous contribution to the Spitfire story had never been covered adequately. In reading some Spitfire books, one would hardly know that Canadians were in the cockpit at all.

Many of the stories that might have been included in this book cannot be told. Some were lost when so many pilots were killed during the war. The passage of decades has taken others. This book is a unique collection of the remembered stories of those who remain. Their recall of the events and of their thoughts and emotions is excellent, and has if anything, benefited from decades of hindsight.

Some still feel regret and anguish over things they should have done; others will never forget those few seconds during which they lost close friends. Yet all remember the joy of flying a Spitfire—a fighter that matched their confident and aggressive spirit. This brilliantly designed airplane was something special in its time. So were—and are—those who built, maintained, and flew it. Other aircraft were good, but none was better than the Spitfire. The men and women of Canada who were involved with the Spitfire will always be considered a breed apart.

The stories contained in *Spitfire* are the result of a Canada-wide search for information as well as interviews with the veterans. Most of the photographs are copied from the personal albums of the veterans themselves. Official sources have been used, but most of this book relies on the words of the veterans. "What was it like?" They will tell you in their own unvarnished terms. They believe that no one except those who were there can ever know what they went through. Yet they have tried very hard to put their thoughts into words. They deny they are heroes, but reading their stories will convince you that all of them are.

When I began working on this book, I was fortunate enough to meet A.V.M. Johnnie Johnson, who, when he saw how keen I was, advised me to go after the pilots and ground crew who were still alive, to get the stories from them. "There will be plenty of time to go to the archives for information after we are gone," he told me, in his typical wisdom and candour.

Spitfire is the result of nine years of following that advice. In retrospect, it is clear that the Canadian Spitfire story is best told in the words of those who were directly involved. Canadians flew in the Battle of Britain. They flew in RAF fighter squadrons and in over a dozen RCAF fighter squadrons. They flew Spitfires all through the Second World War and into the 1950s.

Whether it was shooting down enemy bombers over Buckingham Palace in the Battle of Britain or flying across the English Channel to fight the Luftwaffe, Canadians were there. They fought in the heat of North Africa and were the first to land in France. Swarms of German fighters after D-Day did not stop them, and the heavy anti-aircraft guns, which they hated even more, did not break their spirit or prevent their final victory. Canadians even shot down the faster, jet-propelled planes that were their final opponents in the Second World War.

Many Canadians became aces. Others were assigned to duties such as train busting and reconnaissance. Sometimes the Luftwaffe didn't even show up, which meant that when they did, the Canadians were spoiling for a fight.

Many I talked to said they had read about the First World War flyers when they were children. And many had built model airplanes, just as kids do today. So they had a keen sense of history and a fascination with flying, even before they had the chance to fly. Everyone wanted to fly Spitfires, and the few who were chosen to do so considered themselves lucky

"Johnnie" Johnson and his Spitfire IX, JEJ (EN 398), when he was leader of the Kenley Canadian Wing, July 1943. – "Johnnie" Johnson

indeed. Many were able to recall the tactics and deeds of the men they had read about when they were younger. Some went on to make new rules, helping to develop the science of air fighting and gunnery that is still applied in today's air combat.

Canadians can be proud of the role these men played at a young age in a difficult and faraway conflict. "It seemed like all the world was shooting at us, trying to kill us, for no reason, when we were so young," one said.

Fifty years later, as restored planes pass over airshow audiences, the smooth, rounded beauty of the Spitfire and the low, throaty roar of the Rolls-Royce Merlin engine still evoke strong sentiments among Canadian veterans. They were there—the Canadians—and they were second to none.

These stories will remain as a testament to the courage of Canadian Spitfire pilots and ground crews—a monument to those who survived and those who did not.

The Battle of Britain

Keith "Skeets" Ogilvie, D.F.C., 609 Squadron

THE Battle of Britain was a very intense time—people came and went, you know. You'd lose some. You'd get to know a guy pretty well, then all of a sudden he wasn't there any more. You just sort of got used to it. We had some guys who came to the squadron, and went missing on their first trip. You just didn't know—if your luck ran out, it ran out.

I was in England in 1939, and trained at Hullavington. I was posted to the instructors' school at Upavon but was soon reassigned to 609 Squadron at Middle Wallop in August of 1940. It was a short war for me, but a busy one while it lasted. I flew some three hundred missions before I was shot down in July 1941. You had to be lucky. You could be good, or you could be lucky—I would rather be lucky.

I must have been one of the luckiest. I was one of the few Canadian Spitfire pilots in the Battle of Britain. Most flew the Hurricane. The Spitfire Mark I version that I flew originally had a two-bladed prop, and once we got the three-bladed prop, it was a different airplane to fly. It was faster, and twice as manoeuvrable. It made a difference in the Battle of Britain.

On September 7, 1940, there was a scramble. Hundreds of Jerry bombers were reported over Dover, coming in from Calais, with more coming up the Thames estuary. They were headed for London. We took off to intercept and started our climb to 25,000 feet. In a few minutes, as we approached London, the controller told us we should be able to see them. I was looking all around the sky and couldn't see a thing.

Our C.O. (S/L Horace Darly) led the attack. He said, "OK, 609, beam attack. Go!" He wheeled over and I did a roll as we all followed him down. That's when I gasped. I saw what looked like the whole German air force. I nearly wet myself. I remember they looked like lines of big black beetles—with big black crosses on them.

My God, they were everywhere. We were diving so fast that as I prepared to fire, I realized I had already gone straight through a formation without firing a shot. Not a great start! So, I climbed back up to have another go. Right then, two Me 109s skidded right inside me, not more than 25 yards away. We were all looking down at the bombers. I turned my nose toward them and fired, trying to hit the one in front, but it was the second guy I hit. He flipped over and down, glycol streaming from his engine. Had they come up the other side and seen me first, it would have been me, not one of them going down. But I got a claim for my Messerschmitt.

My most memorable experience of the Battle of Britain happened on September 15, 1940. My logbook shows I was flying PR-F, serial X4107. I was involved in shooting down a Dornier 17. A Hurricane pilot and I were both to claim the bomber destroyed afterwards. This happens from time to time—the bomber had been attacked already, and he'd been damaged. He'd fallen out of formation, probably when the first Hurricanes attacked.

When I saw this bomber limping along, I lit into him, and when I was finished with him, he started to come apart, and spun down. So, it was possible that six different guys could have claimed him, really. That happened. You couldn't sort of isolate one guy and cut him out of a formation, you just had a crack at anything that was moving.

Anyway, that was the bomber that crashed into Victoria Station. A couple of weeks later, the squadron had a letter from Air Force Headquarters. Queen Wilhelmina had watched the combat from her balcony at Buckingham Palace and wanted to have her congratulations sent to the pilot. Because I had film in my Spitfire camera, I got some pictures of the crash. Even though I was given credit for it, it could have been the work of three guys.

The aircraft that I flew most often was PR-F. A few years ago, when I went to the Battle of Britain Museum at Hendon, I was charmed to find that the Spitfire on display was painted up in 609 Squadron colours, and coded PR-F. It gave me quite a feeling to see this aircraft.

I was credited with shooting down four aircraft during the Battle of Britain, and went on to a total of seven and a half (the half being a shared victory).

In the RAF we were taking heavy casualties. We were on our last legs when it came to a close and the Germans changed their tactics, giving us the whole winter to build back up again.

[Note: Records show that the bomber, a Dornier Do 17Z from I/KG 76, was attacked several times. Flown by Oblt. Robert Zehbe, the Dornier was possibly hit first by anti-aircraft fire and may have fallen behind the main formation. It then came under attack by Hurricanes from 310 (Czech) Squadron, and the port engine caught fire. It is believed that Hurricanes from 504 Squadron flown by P/O P.T. Parsons and P/O R.T. Holmes also had a shot at the hapless bomber before Keith Ogilvie finished it off.]

609 Squadron, Biggin Hill, August 1940.
Left to right: Keith Ogilvie of Ottawa; Tom Rigler and Ken Laing of British Columbia. – AP Keith Ogilvie

The Battle of Britain

Jan Zurakowski, 234, 609 Squadrons
(Avro Arrow test pilot)

During 1940 I was in England with Keith Ogilvie, or "Ogi" as we called him, in 609 Fighter Squadron. Earlier, I was with Stew Young in 234 Squadron.

At that time, I was a pilot officer, and so I flew any aircraft that was available. According to my logbook, I carried out eight sorties on Spitfire Mark I No. 4182 and 13 sorties on No. 3191.

From August 14, 1940, to September 11, when 234 Squadron operated from Middle Wallop near Salisbury, we suffered such heavy losses that what remained of the squadron was moved back to St. Evel (Cornwall), and only one section was fully operational. In October I was posted back to the Middle Wallop RAF station and joined 609 Squadron, where Ogi was my section leader.

My first Spitfire flight was at No. 5 Operational Training Unit at Aston Down, on July 24, 1940. On the second flight, I was instructed and authorized to do "aerobatic." Ten days later, I was posted to an operational squadron. After my first flight there, with a bit of aerobatics over our airfield, I was called to the station commander, who furiously explained to me that to do aerobatics on a Spitfire, one needed 50 hours' experience on the type, plus written permission from the station commander.

My poor English (Polish was my first language) and the evidence in my logbook that I was cleared for aerobatics saved my skin.

One problem with aerobatics on the Spitfire was in spinning. The proper technique for spin recovery was described in the Pilot's Notes, though spinning was not recommended. I determined that it was not possible to stop a spin in exactly the required direction. Training did not improve the situation.

I was disappointed because on the old Polish PZL XI fighter I could stop, after any number of spin turns, in the exact desired direction. I later discovered that probably the only time a pilot could be faster than a flying Spitfire was in bailing out of the aircraft in a spin.

I discovered this during a sortie on August 24, 1940. I was attacking a formation of Do 17 bombers that were on a bombing run of Southampton harbour. After my attack, I made the error of climbing to join the squadron. Some of the escorting Me 109s managed to put a few cannon shells into my Spitfire. I lost control of elevator and rudder. My Spitfire then went slowly into a turn, stalled, and ended up in a flat spin.

Having no controls, I had to bail out. At about 18,000 feet I slid open the canopy, climbed out of the cabin, and jumped. I soon found I was descending faster than the Spitfire, which was spinning above my head. I was afraid to pull the rip cord to open the chute because that would have slowed me down, risking a collision with my spinning Spitfire.

The ground was approaching fast, and when I could distinguish a man standing in a field with a gun, I decided to pull the rip cord. It was now or never! My parachute opened immediately. My Spitfire just missed me and hit the ground with a bang. A few seconds later, I landed on the field, next to the old man (from the Home Guard) who was armed with a double-barrelled shotgun. He was badly shaken by the crash.

Suspecting that I might be a German, he asked me if I spoke English. Since my English was poor, I decided to remain quiet. I tried to show him my RAF identity card, but his hands were shaking so violently that he could not take it. I decided to start packing my chute, and soon a British army officer arrived and cleared up the situation.

A Spitfire's vertical speed in a flat spin was fairly low, so the damage to my Spitfire on impact with the ground was not severe. The main engine mounting failed and there was evidence of two gunshots (probably 20 mm calibre) in the rear-fuselage tail junction and one in the port wing.

I learned later that on that day, seven RAF and seven German aircraft crashed on the Isle of Wight. The spot where I landed was not too far away from the spot where, on August 15, an Me 110 was badly damaged by my attacks and crash-landed. The pilot was killed, and the injured gunner was later a prisoner of war in a camp in Canada.

Next morning I returned to my squadron. I was flying again, but learned from my friends in London that I had been officially killed. I had to send a report to the effect that I was very sorry, but that since the date of the crash, I had carried out six operational sorties in August, so I was obviously alive. Shortly afterward, I received two letters addressed to me, marked "Killed in Action" on the envelope. I kept those letters as souvenirs.

During the Battle of Britain, I often used spins to save my life. I can think of at least four times when this simple but dramatic manoeuvre of pretending to be shot down came in handy. I used it when I was attacked by German fighters and had no chance to fight successfully. I usually started with a snap roll, which culminated in a vertical stabilized spin. I would quickly close and open the throttle, producing black smoke from the engine exhaust.

To German pilots, a spin was an indication that the Spitfire was out of control. Black smoke confirmed that the aircraft had been shot down. Why follow and confirm the crash if it meant losing height over enemy territory? Better to claim one Spitfire shot down!

Evidence after the war indicates that German fighters claimed the destruction of three times more RAF aircraft than actual RAF losses in combat. So I was spinning happily, recovering at 5,000 feet or so, and if there was enough gas and ammunition, I would climb again in search of better fighting opportunities.

One might wonder why anyone would use this manoeuvre. There were situations, especially in the Battle of Britain, where we were so outnumbered that the Spitfire had no chance. The manoeuvrability of the Spitfire was so superior to the Me 109 that in a dogfight I considered two or even three Me 109s equal opponents. A section of four Me 109s normally had a smart leader and would generally decline a dogfight. Instead, they would spread widely in all directions, and I would immediately be in good position to open fire on any enemy. However, another Me 109 would also be in a good position to open fire on me, and then I would have to break the engagement.

Above 5,000 feet I could not outdive or outclimb the Me 109, so if my Spitfire's superior manoeuvrability could not be used, pretending to be shot down was a good strategy, saving both the Spitfire and me for the next fight. At low altitudes, with emergency engine boost, the Spitfire allowed for three minutes of extra power, and was definitely better all-round in performance than the Me 109.

I gained a lot of experience on Spitfires. I made over 1,000 flights in 15 different marks, from the Mark I to the Mark 24, while I was in the RAF and the Polish Air Force in England. In 1940, RAF fighters saved Britain from Hitler's invasion. Without air superiority, the Germans could not succeed, even with the colossal strength of their armies.

THE BATTLE OF BRITAIN

J.S. "Stew" Young, 234 Squadron

I flew the Spitfire I and the Spitfire Ia. They had the radiator on one side only. When you got into a fast and powerful dive (350 miles an hour and up), that right-hand radiator gave you a hell of a lot of torque. You had to fly with the stick hard over to the left to counteract the drag caused by the radiator. The later models had two radiators, one on each side, which balanced out the steering. The fastest I ever went was 410–420 mph in a dive. But then I popped my ears, so I had to slow down.

On Friday, October 18, 1940, during the Battle of Britain, I was sent up on a dawn patrol in Spitfire R 6983. As soon as I became airborne, I selected gear up, but nothing happened—the red light didn't come on to indicate the gear was up, and the green light didn't come on to show it was down. At about 140 miles an hour, the gear was hanging there with the right-hand gear half-blocking the radiator. I could only go so fast, otherwise the temperature would start to climb, and once you boiled glycol in a Merlin, you'd had it. So I just stooged around until there was enough daylight to land by. They didn't put flare paths on in those days because the Germans were still around. I guess I was sweating a little bit, wondering if the Jerries were going to pounce me. When it was light enough, I came in. As I crossed the boundary fence, I cut the power, cut the fuel off, and deadstick landed the thing on the runway. It held up for a while, but as the wings lost their lift, the right-hand gear collapsed and I swung around in a big circle. The blood wagon was there—we nicknamed the ambulance that—and the firetruck was there. I just stepped out and said, "Sorry boys, no business this time!"

This Spitfire IIa (P7350) flew in 266 and 603 Squadrons during the Battle of Britain, 1940. The aircraft is still flying today with the Battle of Britain Memorial Flight in England. – Robert Bracken

R.S. Tuck's Last Flight

Al Harley, 401 Squadron

WEDNESDAY, January 28, 1942, dawned like many days at Biggin Hill—some sun, some clouds, and the forecast of rain later in the day. January had been fairly inactive due to the weather. We flew mostly training flights with a few convoy patrols thrown in. The boys were getting itchy for some action, and finally around nine o'clock we were called to the briefing room. A fighter sweep was laid on for over the Channel. This was carried out with nary a German in sight, and we returned to base rather disappointed. After refuelling we were sent off on another sweep, this time over France to Saint-Omer.

A few skirmishes developed on this sweep but nothing of note. After landing, we went to the mess for a very late lunch. The weather was closing in and a light rain had started to fall. I sat at a table with our wing commander and six other pilots and the conversation naturally turned to the weather.

"All is not lost," our wing commander stated. "It is a perfect day for a rhubarb, that is, if there are any volunteers." Seven hands were raised, including mine. Rhubarbs were sneak intrusions, usually by two aircraft, to attack ground targets. We carried them out when the cloud level was low.

In the nine months since I joined the squadron I could not recall a rhubarb being carried out. The fighter sweeps, bomber escorts, and convoy patrols were becoming a bit boring, and the thought of a rhubarb was exhilarating. We decided to cut cards to see who would accompany the wing commander, and my king of hearts was high. I was the envy of the group.

Our wing commander was Robert Stanford Tuck, D.S.O., D.F.C., and two bars. His official count was 29 confirmed victories plus numerous probables and damaged aircraft. At the time, he was the leading ace in the RAF on active duty. He was 26 years old and handsome, with a long scar running down his right cheek—a legacy from a prewar flying accident. His close friends called him Bob, but we addressed him as "sir."

He was a real veteran, respected for his flying abilities, and a leader both on the ground and in the air. He had been shot down four times and was fearless behind the controls of a Spitfire. If I'd ever had the choice to fly with another pilot on a rhubarb, this would have been the man.

"OK, Harley," he said, "let's go down to Intelligence and find ourselves a target."

By the time we arrived at Intelligence, the rain had stopped but there was still a complete cloud cover with a 600-foot ceiling. F/L DeLarose, the intelligence officer, thought we were out of our minds to fly on an afternoon like this. However, he picked out a distillery at Hesdin, France, for our target. The Germans used distilleries to bolster their supplies of aviation fuel, and a few well-placed cannon shells would put this one out of production for months. He showed us photographs of the distillery and the tanks surrounding it.

I was elated in anticipation of my first rhubarb. The Spitfires we were flying were Mark Vb's. Tuck's aircraft (P8783 coded RST) was always in top-notch condition and was just a little faster than the run-of-the-mill Spitfires. Having just been made flight commander of B Flight, I was authorized to sign out my own aircraft. I signed out a Mark VI Spitfire (AA851 coded YO-I) that had been loaned to the squadron for experimental purposes. This aircraft was not supposed to be used on operations but, since it had a souped-up engine, it was faster than our Mark Vb's. I would have no difficulty keeping up with Tuck now.

Tuck was waiting for me at the end of the runway when I arrived. He immediately raised his hand as the signal to open the throttle. The extra power in the Mark VI's engine was obvious as I almost ran past Tuck's aircraft on takeoff. Airborne, flying at low level, we headed for the south coast of England. For me this was the real thrill of flying—skimming the treetops, cruising at 250 miles an hour and watching the towns whiz by. As I flew in a loose formation on

F/L A.E. Al Harley in his Spitfire Mark VB, serial W3131, named DO II *for his wife Dorothy. Biggin Hill, Kent, April, 1942.* – A. E. Harley

Tuck's wing, I thought that this was the ultimate thrill I had been waiting for—flying with a renowned ace of the RAF. Just the two of us.

As we passed the Cliffs of Dover, we dropped down to 50 feet above the English Channel. A few minutes later we were approaching the beaches at LeTouquet with their deserted hotels. The German coast defences were clearly visible as we crossed the beach but, strangely, they did not seem to be manned. Heading inland, we set course for Hesdin.

"Gun sight on," ordered Tuck as he broke radio transmission silence. "Be alert and keep an eye on our tails."

The sound of his voice brought me back to reality. As we flew over the French countryside, farmers in the fields waved at us as if in greeting. I wondered about what mixed feelings they might have had, but it seemed they were glad to see us. Suddenly we came upon a convoy on a country road, nine or ten trucks that appeared to be carrying supplies and a few troops. Tuck dove on them and I followed. I had my gun button turned to the "all guns" position, which meant that when I pressed the trigger I fired two 20 mm Hispano cannons and four 303 Browning machine guns. This was the first time I had witnessed the firepower of the Spitfire in air-to-ground firing. In air-to-air combat you rarely see the concentrated firepower of these aircraft.

The results were devastating. Parts of the trucks flew in all directions as drivers and troops dove for the ditches. Several of the trucks blew up as we hit the gas tanks. Although we made only one pass at the truck convoy, we left a sorry mess behind.

A few minutes later we were approaching a small airfield. We took one pass at it and left several aircraft in flames and set fire to the hangar. Boy, this was great, this was fun. It was stacking up to be everything that I thought it would be. The airfield defences were either sound asleep or nonexistent up to this point. Not a shot had been fired at us.

I had a feeling of complete security. If things got sticky, we had the security of a solid cloud cover just a few hundred feet over our heads. Up till now we had remained at a very low level and the only way we could be plotted was by ground observers. Since they were aware of our presence by this time, our main worry was the German anti-aircraft batteries, although German fighters could not be ruled out.

Tuck was one of the few fighter pilots in the RAF allowed to choose his own code name for radio communications. For a long time he had

Hugh Godefroy of 401 Squadron flying a Spitfire V, YO-X (AD 234), with the name Gerfalcon Emmetts *on the cowling. In March 1942, it was flown regularly by S/L Douglas.* – DND PMR78-108, A.E. Harley

used the name "Bobbie." On this flight, he was Bobbie One and I was automatically Bobbie Two. It sounded a bit sissy to me, but who was I to argue?

We were now approaching our target at Hesdin. Ahead was a long, high ridge of ground. "Bobbie Two, be ready to pull up over that hill and come line abreast," called Tuck.

I put on some throttle and pulled up beside him as we climbed toward the top of the hill. The elevation carried us almost to the base of the low cloud cover. There was our target straight ahead. It looked exactly like the pictures that "Spy" had shown us in the intelligence room at Biggin Hill. There were several large storage tanks beside the plant and several long, low buildings that looked like army barracks.

Each of us picked a tank as our target, and being a novice at this game, I opened fire just a little out of range. Within one or two seconds I was within range and my blast hit the tank square on. With every fourth shell in the cannons being an incendiary, the tank exploded in a ball of fire and black smoke. Tuck hit his target at the same time with the same result. He also raked one of the barrack buildings, setting it on fire. I thought to myself, "Now why didn't I think of that?" but it was too late. The attack had taken the ground defences by surprise, but now the anti-aircraft guns opened up on us as we completed our run. The anti-aircraft fire looked like a lot of red-hot tennis balls coming at us. Some went over our heads, some to the side. Luckily, they scored no hits.

Not wanting to press our luck, we headed north along a highway to find the coast and get back to England. The weather was closing in now, with rain spattering the windscreen. Up ahead we could see a long ridge of ground with tall steel pylons carrying high-tension wires running along it. This would be great fun—to knock off a few insulators and watch the multi-coloured sparks fly across the countryside. I lined up one of the towers in my gunsight and in doing so caught a glimpse of a large transformer at the base of the next tower. Instinctively, I swung to the right and lined up the transformer in my gunsight. In doing so I failed to notice a large tree in my line of flight.

Concentrating on my gunsight, I let go a blast of fire at the transformer just as the tree loomed up in front of me. It was too late. I quickly pulled up but caught the tree 10 feet from its crown. There was a heavy jolt; the aircraft shuddered for a few seconds but continued on. I thought, This is it. In a few seconds my motor will quit, and I had better look for a spot to land.

"Bobbie One, I just hit a tree and may have to land," I called to Tuck.

"Carry on and do your best, Bobbie Two," came the reply. He seemed almost unconcerned. I was hastily checking my engine instruments. Everything seemed normal. The weather was cold and there was no heat in the aircraft, but I had broken out in a cold sweat.

Over the ridge, we found ourselves approaching a large industrial area. This could only be Boulogne, the last place we wanted to be. Our original plan had been to come out south of Boulogne, as the area from Boulogne around to Dunkerque was heavily defended with anti-aircraft guns. Instead of retreating in the direction we came, Tuck decided to skirt the city and hit the coast north of it.

As we swung east all hell broke loose. Anti-aircraft guns opened up on us from all directions. They were well concealed and we had flown into a nest of them. With Tuck flying ahead of me, they concentrated their fire on his aircraft. Amid the hail of fire, Tuck broke right and I broke left. As Tuck broke away, I saw glycol coolant streaming from his engine and knew he had been hit. I circled right, well away from the gun posts, looking for Tuck's aircraft.

"Bobbie One, this is Bobbie Two, do you read me?" No answer. After several calls, I feared the worst. Still circling, I could find no trace of his aircraft. Another A.A. gun opened up on me and this convinced me that I should get the hell out of there.

Banking right to head west, I found myself entering a small valley, at the bottom of which was a stream that could only run to the sea. Staying at treetop level, I followed the valley. In the distance I could see the English Channel. Approaching the Channel, I could see the outline of a gun post. With plenty of ammunition left, I lined up the gun post in my sights.

Fortunately for me, their gun was pointed toward the Channel, and as it swung around, they only had time for a short burst, which went over my head. The gun post was now within range, and I fired everything the Spitfire could muster. The first part of my burst hit mud and the gun crew disappeared as if swept away by a large broom. I flew through the spray of mud as I passed a scant few feet overhead.

My aircraft was now over the Channel, and I knew I would draw fire from every coastal gun in the area. Anti-aircraft shells were bursting all around me. This was when my training served me well. I carried out a "jack-rabbit"—up 200 feet for a few seconds and then down 200 feet for a few more seconds. With the throttle wide open it did not take long to get out of range, although it seemed an eternity.

Finally clear of the coast and with England in sight, I had a nervous reaction I had never experienced before. I was still in a cold sweat and my feet were shaking on the rudder bar. As hard as I tried, I could not keep my feet from shaking. This passed in a few minutes. I was then startled to hear my code name on the radio.

"Bobbie Two, this is base. Is Bobbie One with you?"

"Hello base. No, Bobbie One is not with me."

Five minutes later I circled Biggin Hill airfield and received permission to land. As I taxied toward the dispersal area, I wondered what would happen when they discovered that I was flying the Mark VI experimental aircraft. I anticipated the worst. Standing at the edge of the taxi strip were the station commander, G/C Barwell, the squadron C.O., S/L Douglas, the intelligence officer, F/L "Spy" DeLarose, and an S/L from headquarters. Trying to look nonchalant, I waved to them as I taxied past. News travels fast, and most of the squadron pilots were watching grimly.

I taxied to the parking bay, turned the aircraft around, shut down the engine, and climbed out of the cockpit. A sorry mess greeted my eyes when I inspected the aircraft. The fairing around the radiator was missing as well as one fairing from the undercarriage. The air scoops were plugged with small pieces of branches from hitting the tree. The leading edges of the wings were dented and the aircraft was covered with mud. The engineering officer, F/O Art Warner, a good friend of mine, was on hand. I asked him if he would repair the aircraft and say nothing about it. He agreed.

I threw my parachute over my shoulder and trudged to the dispersal. This, I thought, could be the end of my air force career. For the next hour I answered questions about what had happened and filled out an official report. The loss of Tuck was a major blow to Fighter Command, and they wanted the particulars. Luckily for me, with the fuss over Tuck being shot down, no one noticed that I had been flying a Mark VI.

This was without a doubt the most exciting

operation that I had been on overseas. It lasted just over an hour, but that hour had been packed with thrills and anxiety, as well as sorrow over the loss of Wing Commander Tuck. The following night on the German radio broadcast it was confirmed that Tuck had been taken a prisoner of war. This was a great relief to all in the squadron and to the air force in general.

The next time I met Bob Tuck was in Toronto in the early 1960s. I attended the premiere of the film *The Battle of Britain*, and Bob was there. He had been a technical adviser on the film. He was as enthusiastic and personable as ever, and told me what happened to him on that day. He had lost his engine after being hit and prepared for a forced landing in a small field. As he approached the landing site he saw a motorized gun carrier in the field, and with the ammunition he had left he gave it several quick bursts. On landing, he smashed his nose on the gunsight. When the German soldiers rushed his aircraft, he thought they would probably shoot him. However, he was taken prisoner and spent the next three years in a prisoner-of-war camp.

I will always remember him giving me the most memorable day of my life.

Spitfire V, AE-A (BM 257), the personal aircraft of S/L Bob Morrow (left) from Alberta and Norm Bretz (right) from Toronto. Bretz would soon succeed Morrow as S/L of 402 Squadron. Both would rise to the rank of wing commander during the war. – DND PL 7795

The Search for Paddy Finucane

Bob Morrow, D.F.C., 402 Squadron

On September 8, 1941, at Southend, I flew a Spitfire for the first time. It was a visiting aircraft. Like all pilots, I found it remarkable—very responsive, and light compared to the Hurricane, which was the aircraft 402 Squadron used at the time.

On March 8, 1942, 402 Squadron moved to Colerne (outside of Bath) to reequip with Spitfires. This was in response to a lot of bitching on my part about still flying Hurricanes. On February 14, the commander-in-chief of Fighter Command, then Sir Sholto Douglas, visited us at Warmwell, Dorset. Two days later we made a notable attack with Hurricane bombers on five destroyers, probably sinking one and damaging another. He must have liked what he saw, because he gave us 22 brand-new Spitfire Vb's. I had been expecting some clapped-out old Spits for conversion purposes.

A week later, on March 17, 1942, we moved to Fairwood Common outside of Swansea in South Wales, and took up ordinary duties—we had some fun there. The Irish were suspected of refuelling German subs at the Saltee Islands off the southeast coast of Ireland, and we often patrolled looking for any suspicious activity. A great opportunity to beat up the local countryside. One smart-ass (not from my squadron, thank God) lost his Spitfire when he landed and could not restart his engine.

On May 16, 1942, we moved to Kenley, Surrey, and set about serious business. On May 31, we moved to Redhill in the Kenley Sector.

At that time, Paddy Finucane, D.F.C., D.S.O., was the leading RAF ace. We were at Redhill together and we became good friends. He had a lot of charm and would often take the time to drop by 402 Squadron dispersal to chat with the airmen, much to their delight.

In July 1942, Paddy left to take over the Hornchurch Wing. On July 15, while on a low-level operation over France, in a Spitfire Vb, he was hit in the radiator and started to lose coolant. He managed to get off the French coast and belly-land in the Channel. The RAF or RN sent out three gunboats to try to rescue him. Unfortunately, belly-landing in water almost never worked. The aircraft would pitch into the water, and then it was goodbye.

402 Squadron was off duty. We were called by 11 Group Sector Control, who advised us that the rescue boats were in trouble and under attack by Focke-Wulf 190s, the newest German fighters. We volunteered to help, and the pilots raced to the airfield. Time was vital. Twelve of us managed to take off, in a loose gaggle, as soon as our engines could be started. We took off from our base, which was still at Redhill, and headed straight for the French coast—near Fecamp, as I recall, in the Seine estuary. My logbook shows I was flying my usual Spit Vb, AE-A (BM 257).

From a long distance away I could see one of the motor gunboats already on fire. The FW 190s were diving on the other boats, and I wanted to put a stop to that. We were practically flying on the deck when the FWs suddenly broke cloud above us and dived to the attack. We flew in a defensive circle as the enemy fighters came down in pairs and groups of four, attacking us and the boats.

F/Sgt. Hughes (BM 296) was my No. 2. At one point a 190 attacked us both. I half-rolled into and over it, but Hughes was not so fortunate. Over the R.T. I heard him say that he was on fire. He was barely 100 feet off the water, too low to bail out. Immediately, the nose of his Spitfire pointed straight up. As he undid his safety straps, he was hurled free, parachute billowing out. The rescue boys fished him out of the drink into one of the gunboats below.

There never was a letup. I never put in such a crowded 25 minutes in all my life. I was able to make three separate attacks on the 190s—one at full deflection, which was seldom successful, and another from astern, but at too great a distance. The third was different. I saw a 190 climbing from an attack on the boats.

Spitfire mobile canteen truck from 402 Squadron, 1942. – DND PL 7797

We were close to head-on, and I don't think he saw me. I fired a five-second burst with both 20 mm cannons and four machine guns. Pieces of 190 scattered all over.

As the fight wore on, the Germans seemed to lose their enthusiasm. They never succeeded in breaking up our circle, and eventually they just buzzed off.

When we returned, I found that the cover of my cine-gun had not been removed, such was the haste of our departure, so I never put in a separate claim for my FW. We were always sensitive about putting in any claims that might be considered exaggerated.

During the fight, one 190 was seen to crash into the sea. Another skimmed low over the water, and seconds later only a foamy wake remained. We just never had the time to really check how many dead Germans there were, when there were so many live ones around.

It had been a wild fight. F/Ldr. Brownie Trask (BM 135) had counted sixteen 190s coming at us at one point. F/Sgt. Keene (BM 519) drew smoke from one of them. J.C. Bayly (AR 396) said it seemed as if he had one wingtip continually on a mast, and that it was definitely a vicious circle while it lasted. Sgt. McGraw (BM 698) had some bullet holes in his Spitfire as souvenirs, while P/O Dewar (BM 262) was seriously wounded. Hughes, my No. 2, was also wounded.

Overall, we had only one regret—that Paddy Finucane, with 31 enemy planes to his credit, was never found.

On August 2, 1942, we were reequipped with Spitfire IXa's. This was a remarkable aircraft that deserves special mention. Until this time, the advantage had been with the aircraft that flew highest and climbed fastest. For that reason, the air war had been moving higher and higher. The Spit IXa had two-speed double-stage blowers (superchargers). It took about 500 horsepower to drive the blowers, but the aircraft could fly higher and, at altitude, climb faster than any other. We routinely flew squadron formations at 35,000 feet plus. One time I tried to see how high it would go. Radar gave me an estimate of 45,000 feet—unpressurized and unheated! The German fighters could not complete with the Spitfire at altitude. With the introduction of this aircraft, the air war was forced to go lower, and the Spitfire IXb, with its single-stage blower, became the standard RAF fighter for a long time.

In August 1942, I was to be given command of an RCAF fighter wing, but first I spent a month in Canada. I was delayed in Canada, because I had volunteered to fly a Boston bomber back to England and wound up crashing in northern Newfoundland, mainly because of icing. Knobby Fee was given command of the wing and was later killed.

When we were at Redhill, I introduced the logo of a red Maple Leaf in a white nine-inch circle. My rationale was that the Poles had their insignia, so why not the RCAF? RCAF Headquarters liked the idea.

Flying the Mark V Spitfire

Ron McGarva, 421 Squadron

I believe I am an original member of 421 Squadron. I completed Operational Training Unit (OTU) at Crosby-on-Eden in April 1942, and was posted to 421. They were supposed to be at Coltishall in northern England, but when I arrived at that station I was advised that 421 had moved to Fairwood Common in Wales. I chased them by train all the way down to Swansea and then to the airfield.

The commanding officer at that time was Fred Kelly. I was in B Flight, and my flight commander was George Hill. My stay in 421 was short-lived. As I understand it, the squadron was in a hurry to get down to 11 Group, and as the members had no real operational experience, about half of us were replaced by experienced Canadians from RAF units. I ended up with an RAF fighter-bomber squadron on the southeast coast and spent an eventful and enjoyable year and a half with it.

My strongest memory of Fairwood Common came from what happened during a formation practice. We were flying in a box of four. I was flying No. 4 in the slot. Goody Goodwin was leading. As we flew over the airfield, the air got a little rough. I was tucked right in under Goody's tail and could see the blur of my propeller just under his tail wheel. Well, a bump of rough air hit me at the wrong moment and I clipped the tail wheel tire right off. We had wooden props on the Mark Vs at that time. My prop shattered and the engine got so rough that I had to shut it down. I could not get back to the airfield, so I had to try to land straight ahead in an open field. I left the gear up and skidded to a halt. In those days, all open fields had poles planted in them to stop the German invasion, and I clipped one with my wing, doing considerable damage.

As a result of this experience, I got to meet a delightful gentleman, Group Captain Acherley,

"All OK? Let's go!" Frank Joyce, 421 Squadron. Not long after this photo was taken Joyce became a P.O.W. – R. Beall

the station commander and one of the famous twins who served so gallantly with the RAF. As I stood at attention in his modest office, looking very sad and disgusted with myself, he said, "Son, when you have pranged as many aircraft as I have, it will be time enough to feel sorry for yourself." I said, "Thank you, sir." Then he sent me on my way.

Letters Home

Norm Bretz, D.F.C., 401, 402, 411, 416 Squadrons

I was born in Toronto, but spent most of my years in Winnipeg, where I attended high school. I returned to Toronto after that, and enlisted in the RCAF early in 1940. I received my wings at Uplands, and as a pilot officer was overseas for Christmas. I flew with 401 Squadron and then with the 402. I became a flight lieutenant and then, just before the Dieppe raid, succeeded Bob Morrow as squadron leader.

These are excerpts from several letters I wrote to my sister Madeline during that time.

"As we are seldom up over an hour and a half, we don't have to dress as warmly as bomber crews. At present, we just wear our uniform, but during the winter, we used to pull on a huge turtleneck sweater, which at one time was white. I have a silk scarf made from a parachute, which is useful for keeping out any little breezes from creeping in around the neck.

"The boots are leather fleece-lined, and come up to the knee. Usually these are more for protection against fire than for warmth. With the heavy boots, of course, I have to wear heavy socks. I've just been wearing summer underwear all along, and it's quite warm enough.

"The gloves are leather gauntlets, and in cold weather, a pair of silk gloves under them. These too, are more for protection from fire, as it's quite warm in the cockpit. Of course, at 25 or 30 thousand feet, it gets quite cool, and then we're glad we have them.

"The helmet has a mask which snaps on over the face and supplies oxygen when needed. It also contains the microphone for the R.T. Whenever we go up, whether over the sea, or not, we always wear a jacket called a Mae West because of its remarkable resemblance. It's filled with kapok, and rubber air pockets, which may be blown up by means of a tube.

"It's always being modified to embody a new safety device, for rescue from the briny, so that by now it weighs about a ton. A floating flash, emergency rations, and tubes of morphine are among the developments, so you can see why it is so important that it always be worn.

"You may have read in the papers of some of our activities since we came south. We have really been quite fortunate, although I have been quite excited at times, but so far haven't had many close calls during this interval—I have just touched wood!

Spitfire IX, AE-U (BS 428), of 402 Squadron, carrying a bomb beneath the fuselage. – Peter Arnold

Norm Bretz sitting in S/L Bob Morrow's Spitfire Mark V (BM 257), just before Bretz assumed command of 402 Squadron. – DND PL 7796

"About a month ago [in December 1941] our C.O. was sent back to Canada, which meant that we all moved up a step, which put me in the position of B Flight Commander. It's a lot of responsibility, not only in the air but on the ground as well, but it's a lot of fun, too."

[Note: Bretz won the D.F.C. for his work at Dieppe. It is reported that his 402 Squadron engaged 12 FW 190s at one time. He flew a Mark IX Spitfire that day.]

S/L Norm Bretz flew this Spitfire IX, (BS 430), which was presented by the Canadian Pacific Railway from public donations to the Spitfire Fund. Bretz flew "N" as his usual aircraft during Day Two of the Dieppe raid and for some time afterward. When the aircraft was passed to 416 Squadron it became "DN-N," the personal aircraft of S/L Foss Boulton. Note the red Maple Leaf on a white disc, and the squadron leader's pennant on the nose. – PA 136892

The Dieppe Raid

Don R. Morrison, D.F.C., D.F.M., 401 Squadron

On June 30, 1942, 401 Squadron moved temporarily from Gravesend to Eastchurch on the Isle of Sheppey in the Thames River, east of Chatham. Although we did not know it, the move was part of the preparation for the Dieppe raid, which was soon postponed until August 19, when the tides and weather were again expected to be favourable.

Eastchurch was a permanent RAF station, and we spent a very pleasant week there. The weather was good and we enjoyed the tennis courts, swimming pool, and so on. We even had batwomen! We were surprised when broad white vertical stripes were painted on our cowlings, making our Spits look like bumblebees. During the invasion of Normandy, in June 1944, similar stripes were painted across the wings of all Allied aircraft. We flew a few operations from Eastchurch and then returned to Gravesend, where we were normally based.

On August 14, 1942, the squadron was moved to Lympne, just west of Folkestone and just inland from Hythe on the Channel coast. Lympne was a prewar aerodrome, famous as the English landing field for Louis Bleriot's first flight across the English Channel in 1909. It was also the scene of Douglas Bader's first flight after the accident that cost him both his legs.

During our stay at Lympne, we were billeted at the home of Sir Phillip Sassoon, one of the pioneers of aviation in England. Sir Phillip held pilot's licence No. 3! We enjoyed our stay in his home, which had splendid rooms and several luxurious sunken bathtubs—a real change from the usual RAF quarters. We did a few normal operations—scrambles, patrols, and the like—from Lympne, but we remained unaware that there was going to be a raid on Dieppe.

On August 17, 1942, 401 Squadron escorted 12 USAAF B-17 Flying Fortresses in a raid on the docks of Rouen—their first raid of the Second World War. They flew at 25,000 feet and dropped their bombs with good results. Many FW 190s appeared, and the squadron broke up and was involved in several different scraps. One 190 destroyed, four probably destroyed, and one damaged were claimed by the 401. I was flying my usual YO-A (BS 119). We had one pilot wounded (F/Lt. Ted Wood, BR 630), one missing (P/O Jack Ferguson, BR 159), and one killed (F/Sgt. Rocky Rowthorn, BR 985). Rowthorn's aircraft had been damaged by gunfire during the fighting over Rouen, and he crashed at Biggin Hill when he tried to land it. He had just turned 18.

On the evening of August 18, 1942, we were briefed by S/L Keith Hodson. This was the first word of the planned raid on Dieppe, and we were all thrilled to learn that we would be flying in support of Canadian troops in the first big raid on occupied France.

We woke up early on the morning of August 19, to the sound of bombs and gunfire from Dieppe, only miles across the Channel from us. We went down to our dispersal and found to our disappointment that the B-17s were not scheduled to bomb Abbeville's airport until 10:15. Our 401 Squadron was to escort them, along with 402 and 611 Squadrons. All of us were flying Spitfire IXs, the new, high-altitude models with blowers that cut in automatically at 19,000 feet. They were also equipped with new, belt-fed 20 mm cannons, a big improvement over the original 5 mm drum-fed cannons. We were keen to get going and were naturally getting quite upset as we watched the other Spitfire squadrons flying over to and from Dieppe.

We finally took off at 9:35. We climbed to 23,000 feet to make rendezvous with the Fortresses over Beachy Head and then headed for France. We encountered medium-heavy flak from the French coast to Abbeville, where it was very intense and bursting close to the bombers, but they maintained formation and kept on course until they dropped their bombs. They then swung to port and headed back for the French coast and the English Channel. In the meantime, since no German fighters

This Spitfire IX (BS 180) was flown at Dieppe on August 19, 1942, by F/S A. Lloyd Sinclair. – Bill Marshall

appeared, we had a terrific view of the bombs bursting on Abbeville's airport. No bombs fell on the runways—they all exploded on the buildings, hangars, and administrative and dispersal areas. This was a major blow to the Luftwaffe, since Abbeville was their main fighter aerodrome in the area, and it was knocked completely out of action for the whole day of the raid.

We stayed with the B-17s until they were safely on their way back across the Channel. Hodson (BS 172) then came on the R.T. and said, "OK, boys—let's go to Dieppe." The four Spitfires in Blue Section, led by F/Sgt. Ed Gimbel (BS 176), and including F/Sgt. Al Sinclair (BS 180), stayed with the Fortresses and escorted them safely back across the Channel, then landed at Lympne to refuel. We stuffed our noses down so that we had built up plenty of speed by the time we arrived over Dieppe. On the way down, we could see the flames, the smoke, and the wakes of the ships circling offshore. As we got close, we could see intense air activity. Red and Yellow Sections split up as they jockeyed for position with the German fighters.

Combats developed quickly, since the sky seemed to be full of 190s and Spitfires. Hodson (BS 172), leading Red Section, saw two 190s, which he attacked with F/Sgt. "Zip" Zobell (YO-S, BS 120). The first 190 went down and was claimed as damaged. The two Spitfires then set course back to Lympne. On their way home across the Channel, they spotted four Dornier 217 bombers heading for Dieppe unescorted by fighters, and Hodson again went in to attack, damaging one. Zobell fired and saw cannon shell strikes on another. His aircraft was badly damaged by return fire, and he was slightly wounded, but he landed at Lympne safely. In the meantime, F/Sgt. Stan Cosburn (BR 986) and Sgt./Pilot Leo Armstrong (YO-C, BS 107) attacked the other two Dorniers, saw cannon strikes on both, and claimed them damaged.

Just as we in Yellow Section arrived over the Dieppe area, I spotted a single 190 some 1,000 to 1,500 feet below me and heading in the same direction. I did a wide, slipping barrel roll to lose height and levelled out about 150 yards behind him. As I closed up to about 25 yards, I opened

Don Morrison from Toronto (left) shows off his new Spitfire, YO-A (BS 119), to Bert Wemp, editor of the Toronto Telegram *and later mayor of Toronto. Wemp had been a pilot during the First World War in the RNAS. Morrison flew this Spitfire at Dieppe with 401 Squadron.*

– Don Morrison

up with a two-second burst of cannonfire. I saw strikes all along the starboard side of the fuselage, and several pieces about a foot square blew off from around the cowling. Just as we both went into a very thin layer of cloud, he exploded with a terrific flash of flame and black smoke. Suddenly, my windshield and hood were covered with oil and there was a terrific clatter as pieces of debris struck my aircraft.

I broke away, as I could not see through my windshield. I slowed down enough to open the hood so that I could have some vision, and then we rejoined the other two aircraft of Yellow Section. As we dove down to about 1,000 feet to head for home, I was unaware that my aircraft had been damaged. I imagine that some of the debris from the exploding 190 had punctured my radiators.

Suddenly the engine started to cough and the aircraft shuddered violently. I realized that I could not make it back across the Channel to Lympne, so I decided to bail out. We had heard that ditching the aircraft in the sea was rarely successful. Paddy Finucane had been killed just a couple of months before when he tried. I pulled up and started to climb, but my engine cut out completely and I only managed to reach about 2,000 feet. I took off my helmet, undid my safety straps, and tried a couple of times, unsuccessfully, to jettison the hood.

I trimmed the aircraft fully nose down and kicked the stick forward, expecting to be shot out like a watermelon seed. Unfortunately, my parachute pack caught on the hood, and I stopped suddenly, hanging out of the cockpit from my hips, looking down over the nose at the Channel, which was coming up very quickly. A really big kick popped me out, and I clipped my forehead on the radio mast as I rolled over backward. I pulled the rip cord immediately, and just in time—the chute opened just before my feet hit the water. If I had been over land, I don't think I would have survived.

As soon as I came to the surface, I released the parachute, inflated my dinghy, and climbed in. Two of our Spitfires, flown by F/Sgt. Bobby Reesor (YO-H, BS 177) and Sgt./Pilot John Chapin (BR 951), circled me, and I waved to say that I was OK. A third aircraft, flown by F/Lt. Jimmy Whitham (BR 628), went to fetch a rescue launch, the RAF *Roundel*, which was not far away.

In the meantime, the two aircraft that had been circling me were running short of fuel. They headed back to Lympne, but not until another squadron came along to circle me until I was picked up, 17 miles off Dieppe, at about 11:10. I raised my flag, and that helped the crew of the launch to spot me quickly. That big black bow approaching at high speed was certainly a wonderful sight!

I was given dry clothes and had the cut over my eye bandaged, and then they wanted me to stay in the bunk in sick bay. There was just too much going on, so I insisted on going up to the bridge to watch the action. I was told that I would have to stay on the boat until it returned to port that night, so I had no hope of rejoining the squadron for the rest of the day's operations.

During that afternoon, we were sent on several other crash calls, but without success.

Often we were operating within sight of the French coast. We spotted a floating mine and tried to sink it with rifle fire from a safe distance, but both the boat and the mine were moving too much, so we had to give up.

We saw an attack by German bombers on the returning convoy beaten back by heavy A.A. fire from the ships. We saw the explosion and pall of black smoke caused by two Spitfires colliding head on. We watched gunfire from the shore batteries being returned by the ships and saw some Bostons and destroyers laying down smoke screens to protect the convoys.

Later in the afternoon, two 190s passed over us at about 5,000 feet. I saw them attack another rescue boat (HSL 122) and, after a thrilling high-speed battle, set it on fire. Knowing that we could not do much with our light armament (303s), our skipper raced back to get help from a small naval patrol vessel (MI 513) that we had seen earlier. As we returned to the burning rescue boat, another was going in to pick up survivors. The previous high-speed battle was repeated until the second boat was also stopped and set on fire. The 190s then began strafing the survivors in the water.

Two Spitfires came out from England and circled us as close as they could. We pointed to the burning launches and to the 190s that were still firing, and they set out to help. I was getting set to watch the battle at close range when six more 190s appeared suddenly and dived to attack us. We scrambled for cover—those winking red gun flashes from their wings scared the daylights out of me. I had just watched them set the other two rescue boats on fire!

The trifling return fire put up by our inadequate Lewis guns did not appear to bother them in the least. Either the bursting 20 mm shells from the naval vessel did or they ran out of ammunition, since they pulled up and headed back to France. Our launch was not damaged too badly, but our radio was knocked out. We pulled over and, with the navy boat, started to pick up the survivors from the two furiously burning launches. Their fuel and ammunition supplies were exploding, and many of the men in the water were screaming with pain. They all seemed badly wounded, and several of us dived overboard to help lift them up the boarding nets. We picked up 14 survivors and the navy boat picked up 4 more—there should have been 22!

Robert Zobell of Alberta was injured at Dieppe in this aircraft, YO-S (BS 120). – Don Morrison

Two Spitfires from 91 Squadron circled us and then escorted us back toward Newhaven at Beachy Head. Since the survivors were so badly wounded, the skipper raced back at full throttle. We saw bombs fall near the convoy, but way off the mark.

As soon as we pulled up to the jetty, the wounded men were put into waiting ambulances, and then we were able to go ashore. At the same time, the first survivors from the beaches at Dieppe were coming in. Until that time we had no idea how things had gone for the troops. We soon found out that they had taken a terrible beating. I was not surprised, because I had flown over and along the cliffs at Dieppe many times and knew that it was a heavily fortified area, defended by shore batteries and heavy concentrations of flak. I was, of course, unaware of the number of defending troops or their firepower.

When I had the opportunity to visit Dieppe many years later, I was appalled when I saw the shale beaches, the sea wall, the exposed and perfectly flat front, and the encircling cliffs. The attacking troops faced unbelievable difficulties on impossible landing areas against well-protected and heavily armed defenders. Our men went ashore with nothing heavier than Bren guns; the units involved in the landing were fortunate to have any survivors at all!

While I was spending the day in my dinghy and on the rescue launch, 401 Squadron took off from Lympne at 13:25 for their second operation over Dieppe. By that time, the surviving troops had withdrawn and the convoy was well on its way back across the Channel. There was still a great deal of activity, as the 190s were following and attacking. In the combats that followed, F/Lt. Whitham claimed one 190 probably destroyed and another damaged. P/O Harold Westhaver (BR 623) claimed one 190 damaged. During this intense fighting, there was no time to follow the damaged aircraft to see if any of them crashed into the sea. As it was, Sgt./Pilot Armstrong was hit and bailed out (he was later taken prisoner). Sgt./Pilot Morton Buckley's aircraft (BS 187) was shot down. Buckley, who was from Fonthill, Ontario, didn't survive the crash.

On the third trip of the day, 401 Squadron took off at 16:50 with only ten aircraft remaining. They patrolled the returning convoy but encountered no enemy aircraft and returned to Lympne.

No story about the Dieppe raid would be complete without a tribute to the men of the Air Sea Rescue Service. On that one day, August 19, 1942, they plucked many airmen out of the Channel to fly again. They did so with tremendous effort, under extremely difficult circumstances, and often while under attack by 190s.

Our squadron had performed many searches for downed airmen in support of the rescue launches. But until I spent that day on HSL 177, I had never realized how difficult their work was. Those men of the Air Sea Rescue Service operated in fair weather and foul, often within sight of the French coast and within range of the German coastal artillery. They had little armament—only Vickers and Lewis guns—and no armour plate.

And let us not forget the crews of the Walrus flying boats, which picked up many men, often under the very noses of the Germans. At times they couldn't take off again because of heavy seas and had to taxi all the way back home—a long and difficult trip, but a welcome one for many downed pilots. This is exactly how S/L Ian Ormston returned to England in September 1943, after his last flight with 401 Squadron.

They were brave and gallant men—some of the true unsung heroes of the war.

DIEPPE

George Aitken, 403 Squadron

RECALLING the events of Dieppe after so many years is not as easy as might be imagined, but a few memories are revived by reviewing one's logbook and studying the duties and personal notes written on the pages where the Battle of Dieppe is recorded.

Dieppe, as we all now know, should have taken place in July. Our 403 Squadron was ordered to Manston. We arrived on July 1, 1942, and remained there until July 8, when we returned to Catterick. On August 16, we were once again made operational and flew to Manston. We had known since our July activity that some type of combined action was anticipated, but we didn't know where it was to take place or just what sort of thrust it would be.

On August 18 some of the 403's pilots carried out normal sweeps and patrols along the White Cliffs, and I was among them. The weather had been good, and Manston was an ideal location at that time of year.

Following the patrol of a convoy in Barrow Deep, we were all mustered for a grand-scale briefing. Most of us had been confined to Manston barracks since arrival, and I don't recall too much about the briefing—only that there were lots of large-scale maps and that we were shown the part we were expected to play in the

Left to right: Sgt. A. Thomas, D.W. Rathwell, F/O Roy Wozniak (in cockpit), Sgt. L.G. Barnes, F/O G.D. Aitken, Sgt. R. Dunbar. S/L Syd Ford flew this Spitfire Vb, KH-P Phyl-Marie (BM 344) at Dieppe while leading 403 Squadron. – Roy Wozniak

S/L Syd Ford of 403 Squadron with his personal aircraft, KH-P (BM 344), Phyl Marie, which he flew at Dieppe on August 19, 1942.
– Roy Wozniak

following day. Most of us left full of anticipation, now that we knew we were to be on an operation of such magnitude.

Our squadron was scheduled for at least four operational flights, which meant that most of us would get on at least two flights. Squadron commanders and flight commanders would, of course, be on as many as they could.

As usual, each of us carried an escape kit and a French money pouch, as well as a revolver. Personally, I was never one for the revolver—it was a most cumbersome item. Most of us kept it in a flying boot, but I had always figured, since my bail-out of June 1942, that I would have only lost it when I took to my chute. Also, although we had practice using them, I was never impressed with their performance, particularly as I was too small to use one well.

I was the squadron's parachute officer, so I inspected all our chutes in preparation for the next day's events. We had been told to get an early night so that we would be well rested for the next day's long activity. I really doubt that many of us had too much sleep. Some of us were busy writing last-minute notes to the people at home, even though we could not mention the activity that we would play a hand in the next day. Others indulged in card games to ease the tension that had now begun to mount.

Then morning came. The raid on Dieppe started quite early for 403. The dispersal hut was a beehive of activity as we all watched to see whose names would go up on the readiness board for the first piece of the action. My suspense was soon relieved when I found that I was to fly as Blue No. 4 (KH-J, BM 594). After being assigned we went to briefing, and then returned to dispersal to ready ourselves for takeoff.

The ground crews were as excited as we were. They had shined our coupe tops to perfection and filled our petrol tanks to capacity. Our aircraft guns were ready to respond to the slightest press on the firing button.

Our main objectives on all flights were to provide cover for the navy, army, and air force bombers, and to try to draw out enemy aircraft for combat before they reached their protective objectives at Dieppe. No. 4 in a flight is not always the best spot to be in. A pilot flying this position has plenty to do. He has to keep an eye on both his flight commander and his No. 2 while keeping his leader covered so that he can provide warning of attacking fighters from above and behind. He has a lot of throttle manoeuvring to do to keep in proper position, and as a result he has to watch petrol consumption. He is a busy bee.

As our squadron approached the French coast I remember seeing smoke, explosions, boats and barges of all shapes and sizes, and, of course, flak coming up from enemy positions. I used to call this flak "roses with black stalks." The flak created a black trail as it came up from the ground and, when it burst, a mass of red would appear within the black cloud. Fascinating, but disastrous to any aircraft that might be in close proximity. Where were the German fighters?

We continued our sweep over Dieppe and made a half-circle, bringing ourselves into a position that would lead us back home again. Still no threats. I remember thinking that perhaps our bombers had caused such havoc at the airfields in and around Dieppe that all enemy aircraft were either destroyed or grounded. However, when I think back today, this was probably good German strategy. They had already met us on the beaches and had been able to hold the assault. They knew that sooner or later we would be forced to retreat, so why waste aircraft and men on eight sightseeing intruders? We would have to go home soon, as our petrol was being sucked up. As we came back over the coast, I recall looking toward Dieppe, now on our left, and thanking my lucky stars that I was in the sky instead of on the ground, where such stiff defences were being encountered by our naval and ground forces.

We landed back at Manston to be met by our faithful ground crew, who hoped to hear words of our fighting exploits. None of us had fired a shot, and only our petrol tanks required refill after our trip of one hour and 40 minutes.

As I recall, the next patrol encountered the same thing we did. (My aircraft, BM 594, was flown on that second run by my friend Roy Wozniak.)

I was scheduled to fly on the next mission, this time as No. 4 in Yellow Section (BM 594 again). We were to provide high cover escort to some Fortresses assigned to bomb fighter fields in the Abbeville area.

After briefing, we took off. From our high vantage point we were able to see Dieppe, still ablaze with smoke and explosions. The Fortresses encountered flak but continued their run. Our squadron commenced its left turn and, being on the outside flank of the wing, it seemed we had to go quite a distance into enemy-occupied territory. Still we encountered no fighters.

Activity went begging, but we did hear a lot of R.T. chatter in our Blue and Red Sections. Unless we ran into difficulty, the rule was R.T. silence at all times, so that we could hear the commands of our leaders. Blue and Red Sections had reported sightings, and we expected to be jumped at any time. Our flight weaved as never before, but we saw no bogies. By this time we were spread out to provide as much cover as possible to the Fortresses, which were now returning from their missions.

Dieppe was much easier to see now, and to me it looked grim. Some of the boats and barges were on end, some upside down. Others looked like they had torn free and lacked the order that I had noticed on my first trip. Some looked as if they were trying to pull out.

Another hour and 40 minutes was soon consumed, and our second flight returned to Manston. I did not get another trip in that day; however, by the end of it, five men in our squadron destroyed or damaged German aircraft. We had lost P/Os Walker (EN 850), Gardiner (AR 439), and Monchier (AR 437), three very fine young Canadians with whom, sadly, I had only a short friendship.

August 20 saw our squadron back in the air, returning to Catterick for more training, replacement pilots, and new aircraft. We all hoped that our efforts at Dieppe would earn us a return posting to full operational service at a southern aerodrome in 11 Group.

S/L R.H. "Kelly" Walker, C.O. of 416 Squadron, sitting on the wing of his Spitfire IX, DN-K (K for Kelly, BS 129), in May 1943. Note that wartime censors have obscured the Maple Leaf–lynx badge of 416 Squadron. – DND PL 15852

City of Oshawa Squadron

R.H. "Kelly" Walker, 416 Squadron

I joined 416 Squadron on June 10, 1942. At that time there were 11 pilots and 18 aircraft. Together with one other new arrival, this made 13 pilots, enough to provide leave to the others. This contrasts with conditions at the end of the war, when there were as many as 50 pilots and many more aircraft.

I decided to impress the others with my flying ability and did a roll over the airfield. Unfortunately, the seat came loose. There I was, "on the grass" (at very low altitude), and upside down with 70 pounds of equipment and parachute pushing me against the canopy. Fortunately, I was able to gain some altitude from the forward momentum of the aircraft. Having done so, I carefully turned over. The seat then dropped back, though it still pressed on the column, making it hard to control the aircraft. By gentle turns, I was able to land. Probably the seat was not firmly reattached when the oxygen bottles were being serviced.

On a formation flight with our C.O., Lloyd Chadburn, I had a problem when the hose connection for my windscreen de-icer broke, and I could not see a thing. I had to pull out of formation and slow down enough to be able to open the coupe top. After that, the designers of the Spitfire eliminated this particular feature, possibly as a result of my experience.

One of my closest calls came when I was still at an Operational Training Unit. According to my logbook, it was April 1942. I was flying a rather war-weary Spitfire when I had a glycol leak. I did not know how long the engine would run but knew it was only a matter of time before it seized. I made it back to base at Aston Downs and was down to 1,000 feet, and in the process of landing, when the engine quit. Smoke came pouring into the cockpit. I was too low to bail out and was losing my air speed. Under 87 miles an hour the Spitfire really mushes in, and I dropped about five feet above the runway. The two legs stuck in a rut and sheared off, and then, with rattles and a big bang, the airframe bounced up on the runway with the engine on fire. I thought it would blow up. As soon as I came to a stop I got out and ran a safe distance away. The firemen pointed to the two legs stuck in the rut before the runway, standing as a monument to my recent escape. A very shaky do!

Most of our flying took us over water. England was virtually a big aircraft carrier. On flights toward the enemy coast, we would fly low to avoid being detected by radar. We always were on the lookout for enemy fighters, and enemy ships seemed to have guns welded on wherever possible. A bigger hazard than any of these soon became apparent.

At first we did not realize how serious a problem birds could be. In the exuberance of youth, I once broke through a flock of birds on purpose, to see what would happen. Fortunately, I missed them all, though some must have gone through my propellor and I recall them shooting past on both sides of my cockpit. Had they hit, it would have damaged my Spitfire and might have landed me in the Channel.

Everyone soon began to realize what a menace these gulls and terns could be. They could put quite a dent in the leading edge of a Spitfire's wing, even though it was heavily reinforced.

Later on, I did have the misfortune of ingesting a bird through the oil cooler. It smashed right through the protective screen and into the engine. All I knew at the time was that my throttle had jammed a bit. I regained control and continued on to France and back, though my kite did not fly right at all. When I landed, the mechanics stripped down the aircraft to discover that the Rolls-Royce Merlin was full of feathers and bird parts. Evidently, it had gone right through the engine. I was doubtless emitting feathers through the ejector exhausts, too. But, triumph of engineering that the Spitfire was, it had brought me back safely.

When attacking trains, we would fly very low to guarantee hits. When they saw us coming, the train crews would jump out of the locomotive, no matter what speed they were going, probably pulling a release valve. They knew we were aiming for the front of the train. On one attack, I was so low I had to pull up over the locomotive. As I did, I could see the engine blowing steam. I was flying through a cloud of stones.

I remember what a curious thing it was. When I landed back at base, no one would believe me when told them the Germans were now throwing stones at us, too. It developed into a small argument. To settle the matter, I walked out to my aircraft and looked it over for evidence.

With my knife, from a deep dent in the leading edge of one wing, I pried out a piece of small black rock. Coal! So that's what it had been! I was going too fast to see if I had actually hit the train. Evidently I had. I must have exploded the boiler on the train, and the force of that had blown coal all over.

After my discovery, a repair crew went over my Spitfire and found a lot more damage, including a much abraded propeller, which had to be replaced, and numerous dents, which had to be repaired.

Sometimes there was equipment failure. More dangerous was complacency; things could become so routine that one made careless mistakes. One such time my No. 2 and I could have both been shot down as the result of my inattention. I had neglected to switch on my oxygen to the proper setting, and when we climbed for height, I became increasingly euphoric and carefree.

It was not like being drunk. I would describe it this way: if anyone had been shooting at me, I would have watched the bullets hit my wings with detached interest. As it happened, two Me 109s were stalking us. I did not order any evasive action; instead I was completely preoccupied with my windscreen which was now unaccountably fogging up. Had my oxygen been properly set, this would not have happened.

My No. 2 was waiting, and depending on me to make some brilliant countermove. I was still wondering whether the fog on my canopy was forming on the inside or the outside. It couldn't be the outside—we were moving too fast. Finally, it seeped into my brain that we had a problem. I looked around to see two of the biggest 109s you ever saw. Why they never opened fire, I don't know. Maybe they were nonplussed by our failure to make a move.

I called out for me and my No. 2 to go stick over into a hard dive, and we pulled underneath the rest of 416 Squadron. The 109s, probably thinking we had been decoys, and now facing superior odds, vanished quickly. As we entered lower altitude, my canopy began to unfog, and so did my thinking. I adjusted my oxygen. Had it not been for the 109s, I would probably not even have known there was a problem.

The 416 was involved with a lot of different missions, including convoy patrol, and interception of unidentified aircraft that had been picked up on radar. We also escorted American and RAF bombers attacking targets in France. In August 1943, amid all this activity, I became C.O. of 416, taking over from S/L Grant, who then took over 403 Squadron.

We made quite a few attacks on Beaumont-le-Roger aerodrome, escorting American Marauders while they dropped their bombs. On one mission, on September 25, 1943 (DN-W, EP 452), we escorted 24 Beaufighters attacking enemy shipping off Holland. A big ship was hit by a torpedo when two Beaufighters went in. We made a number of these anti-shipping strikes, flying over the cold North Sea to Den Helder, which was always very heavily defended.

On October 19, 1943, while I was on another such mission, the prop on my Spitfire (DN-N, AB 203) ran away when the mechanism failed. The pitch control usually allowed for a maximum of 3,000 revs. I was down near the water, to stay under enemy radar and in formation. The control stick was thrashing wildly, and the aircraft was shaking so hard I couldn't see. I throttled back to 4,000 revs—1,000 over maximum—and turned back for England. Once I throttled back, I regained a measure of control, the shaking was not as bad, and I managed to climb up to bail-out height. Somehow I staggered back to Coltishall, where I made an emergency landing.

The North Sea was not always denied victims. In one case I saw a Spitfire pilot down in the water. He was unable to release his tangled parachute and, though he made a heroic effort to keep swimming, it pulled him under. After that, I always made sure I had a knife so that I could cut off my parachute if I had to. In another instance that still baffles me, I saw a pilot safely bail out into the water and get into his dinghy. We circled above and saw him wave. Seeing he was safe, we noted his exact location and departed, as we were low on fuel. We returned in minutes to find the dinghy empty. The waves were not heavy enough to overturn the small rubber raft, but there was no sign of the pilot.

On one rescue mission, with Johnnie Johnson leading the show, I almost ran out of gas. I radioed to him that I was out of gas and headed back to Tangmere. I was down to five gallons, and still over the water…four gallons, I could hardly bear to watch…then, here's the coastline, am I gonna make the airfield?…three gallons, then two…I landed at Tangmere, empty.

Because of the short range of the Spitfire, we would run out of fuel very quickly. I remember another time, at the civilian airport at Croydon, I had an empty gas tank and had to land underneath an aircraft that was taking off.

The station commander emerged in a rage and told everyone that if that bloody Spitfire pilot's story did not check out, and the aircraft took less than 87 gallons to fill, I would be court-marshalled. The little Englishman manning the bowser told me I wasn't 'alf lucky, because they pumped 91 gallons into my Spitfire. There were some angry phone calls, but they probably told him that experienced fighter pilots were in short supply. I flew back to my squadron.

We engaged enemy aircraft fairly often on our missions. On May 13, 1943, during my first tour, I destroyed an FW 190 while flying my Spitfire IX (DN-K, BS 129). It was a typical mission, escorting Mitchell bombers to Boulogne. On that tour, I also accounted for an Me 109 damaged, three trains damaged, and two gun posts shot up. I made 98 sweeps between June 10, 1942, and October 31, 1943, when my first tour of ops ended.

I flew quite a few different Spitfires. We flew Mark Vs, then Mark IXs, then went back to flying the Mark Vs before getting newer Mark IXs. My usual aircraft was DN-K, for "Kelly," but my logbook shows I flew many others.

Chuck Steele of 411 Squadron, with his aircraft on September 1, 1942, at Digby.   – DND PL 10722

Flying the Mark V Spitfire

C.M. "Chuck" Steele, 411 Squadron

I started flying in 1941. I went overseas to join 411 Squadron in August 1942. We flew clipped-wing Mark Vs all during 1942 and 1943.

That picture of me with Spitfire DB-Q was taken in September 1942, when my squadron was at Digby in Lincolnshire. I usually had DB-F. We operated from Digby for the winter, then we went down south to Kenley and Biggin Hill. After that, we went to Kent and lived in tents in 2nd TAF. That's what we did: we were constantly moving.

We did a lot of practice flying, escorting Fortresses and medium bombers, mainly Bostons, over to Europe. The Germans didn't come over to attack us with their bombers much then — they were preoccupied with Russia, so we didn't have much of a problem with them. We went over there to bomb.

They did leave a few of their best fighter squadrons along the Channel, under the command of people like Adolf Galland, and they were very good. Especially the new FW 190s. They were generally considered better than our Mark Vs, although the clipped wings did make us more manoeuverable down lower. They were good to fly—they cut down on the blower, so they got more speed when low—but they weren't as good over 13,000 feet as the normal ones. They had us at 10,000 to 12,000 feet all the time, which was dangerous because of the flak.

We flew many missions over the Channel. Once, we were supposed to escort the British air minister's aircraft but the weather was so bad, we never found him.

On April 14, 1943, our flight commander, F/L Johnston (P8715), was shot down off the coast of Normandy. We had to stay behind and see if we could find him. We didn't have any luck—he was dead, I guess, though a dinghy was spotted. There were six of us, and we continued to look for him for some time.

Suddenly we were jumped by 12 FWs. We lost the C/O (S/L D.G.E. Ball, EP 489); he was shot down. However, C.S. Pope (AD 557) and A.B. Barber (AB 802) shared a victory. A squadron of Typhoons was sent out to help us. They arrived just after the attack, but the Germans must have known they were coming, because they took off—lucky for us!

I went on to fly the Mark IX, which was a big improvement over the Mark V. We considered it a match for the 190s. After my service with 411 Squadron, I became a test pilot at a repair and salvage unit. Our repair and salvage unit repaired the aircraft in Normandy after the invasion. If they were too bad to repair over there, I would fly the aircraft back to England, to Odiham, so they could be repaired at a permanent site.

Those damaged aircraft could be a little dicey, especially over the Channel. Sometimes they were not in good enough shape to fly very far. Sometimes there were problems, like the one time, when the pitot for the air speed indicator was not installed!

When I was due back on ops, the war ended.

MALTA

Noel "Buzz" Ogilvie, 130, 185, 401, 403 Squadrons

In 1942, I was in 130 Squadron in Portreith, England, flying Spitfire Vs. My friend Jimmy Lambert, who later became C.O. of 403 Squadron, volunteered with me for overseas service. We were bored with England because of the lack of action and the dreary weather. The whole squadron was selected shortly thereafter to serve overseas and Jimmy and I got the blame. Our Spitfires were crated, and the squadron was shipped in convoy to Gibraltar.

We test-flew our Spitfires after reassembly, and on May 16, 1942, they were hoisted aboard the aircraft carrier *Eagle*. We were going to Malta, though nobody told us.

Noel Ogilvie – Noel Ogilvie

On May 18 we were in position off Algiers. We had no training in carrier takeoffs but we had an RAF carrier pilot explain how it was done. The distance from Algiers to Malta was about 700 miles—close to four hours' flying time. At about noon, we were waiting in our Spitfires for enough wind to take off.

The Spitfire V did not have adjustable flaps. We lowered our flaps, and the ground crew placed wooden wedges under our wings; we lifted our flaps, and the wedges would give us about 15 degrees of flap. When we got airborne, we would lower the flaps and the wedges would fly off. We would then retract the flaps and proceed to our destination. British ingenuity!

With all those Spitfires on deck, I thought we made a perfect target in an enemy sea. Finally the checkered flag was waved and down the deck we went. Those of us in the lead had a lot less deck than those who followed. We watched our C.O., S/L Bill New, vanish as he made the first takeoff and then reappear. As I weighed less than him, I was sure I would make it. I followed him and saw my prop wash ruffle the water on the way out from the carrier.

On Malta, I was posted to 185 Squadron. Our Spitfire Vs, with Volkes filters, were pitted against the new 109Fs of the Luftwaffe and the Re 2001s and MC 202s of the Italians, as well as hordes of enemy bombers of all types.

There were three main airfields on Malta: Takali, which was a large grass field; Luqua, which had a runway; and Hal Far, which was just an old fruit orchard with most of the trees removed. Every time we took off, we raised the dust something terrible.

On July 2, 1942, I was scrambled with the rest of the squadron to intercept a fighter sweep by the Germans. I flew GL-Z (BR 468) that day. We were sent up to 25,000 feet. The controller thought the enemy was 3,000 feet below us, and as we approached we could see them. What his radar didn't show was that there was a gaggle of 109s above us.

Somebody in our flight of four aircraft saw those 109s and called a break, but my radio had given up, so I didn't hear the command and I dove into the enemy below. Thus I found myself alone with six 109Fs. I was just turning to get a shot at one of them when I was hit by cannon and machine-gun fire.

The hits immediately threw my Spitfire into a spiral dive, with glycol coming out of my engine in brown-black smoke so that I couldn't see. My main objective then was to get the aircraft out of the wild spiral so I could get my canopy open. In such a dive, there's a lot of centrifugal force and it's hard to get out.

Eventually, I got the aircraft out of the dive, and I soon had the canopy open and one leg over the side. At that moment, for some reason, the pall of vapourized glycol shifted so that I could see. I then realized I was only about 1,000 feet from the ground. By the time I could get out and deploy my parachute, I would be too low, so I decided to try and take the aircraft in.

Since the engine was shot, there was no power, but I managed to pump the wheels down by hand, and make a dead-stick landing at Takali airfield. The aircraft looked like a sieve! I was lucky I wasn't hit.

I was just going to head for the dispersal hut when I saw Laddy Lucas, the C.O. of 249 Squadron, waving his arms at me, shouting at me to go back, and pointing up. I didn't understand why until I realized that the 109 that had shot me down was still trying to kill me.

I dove under the aircraft—not the smartest thing to do. I could see his cannon shells going right past, kicking up puffs of dirt, just missing me. Then away he went. Had it not been for Lucas, I might not be here today.

Flying at Malta was an unforgettable experience. Every day was filled with activity and danger. Not long ago I was able to return there and glad to relive some memories without all the stress and tension of those days.

This Spitfire V, GL-E (BR 126), crash-landed in Malta. – Noel Ogilvie

A Woman in a Spitfire

Marion Orr, Air Transport Auxiliary, Ferry Command

OUR training was done on Tiger Moths, Magisters, and Fairchild 24s. In England, when they were satisfied that we could fly, we went on to Harvards, and then Hurricanes. After 30 hours we were ready for the Spitfire.

I was anxious to get on with it. I went into our operations room and over to the table where they put the chits in for the aircraft we were to fly that day. There was the slip for me—a Spitfire Vb, AB 845! I was all excited and could hardly wait to start.

When we arrived at the unit, they dropped me off with my gear. After I signed the papers, an engineer and I drove out to the aircraft in a jeep. It was sitting there, all ready. A real sleek machine—it looked so long from the spinner to the rudder, and had a small, narrow undercarriage. The engineer helped me get in. I slid down and all I could see was instruments; however, he put my overnight bag under my chute, and that did the trick. It was hard on my clothes but at least I could see. He seemed in a hurry to get me out of there.

After I got comfortable, I checked the cockpit with my blue book in hand. While I was checking the controls, I looked at the ailerons and said, "These wings are too short!" He said, "No, it's what they call clipped wings—just a modification. I checked it out this morning, and ran it up just before you arrived." He told me all the good things about them. Then he warned me about the tail lifting up on the run-up, and about how, on a rough field, Spitfires teeter because of their narrow undercarriage.

I started the engine and nearly blew the engineer off the wing. He said, "Do your takeoff check while taxiing." I felt like a one-armed paper hanger trying to keep it straight. I was all over the place but managed to swing it around, and down the centre line, while making sure everything was in order. It put me in mind of a high-spirited horse waiting to leave the starting gate.

Being an older machine, it had only one cooler, and that was back of the undercarriage on the left side. Then I remembered what he said—that it will overheat if you sit too long—and opened the throttle. I was pressed right back in the seat. I thought I was going to end up in the tail as the trees down both sides of the runway became a blur. When I eased back on the control, the plane shot into the air like a homesick angel. What a sensation! I felt like I'd been shot out of a gun!

At 5,000 feet, I began to get my senses back. The first thing I did was look down. Then I set everything according to the blue book, and circled around the vicinity, getting my thoughts together, till finally I had 100 percent control.

I thought to myself, this is really flying. The air was smooth and the engine was purring at 210 miles an hour, which to me was fast. I had added about 20 minutes to my ETA, so as I neared Cosford I went to a practice area and did a few things to get the feel of it some more. Then I joined the circuit with the rest of the aircraft and got the green light from the control truck at the end of the runway. As luck would have it, I hardly felt the landing.

Spitfire was a perfect name for that aircraft and there will never be another like it. The last one I flew was BL 665. We were not supposed to take cameras with us, but since this was my last flight, and it was going to be scrapped, I snapped a picture. I felt quite sad. Yet it was good to see the end of the war.

ATA ferry pilot Marion Orr, shown here with a Spitfire V (BL 665), flew many different Spitfires during the war. – Marion Orr

AU-G (BR 138), the Skychief II. – R.H. Beall

Pilot Richard Beall by the nose of AU-G Skychief II *(BR 138). Note the unusual cowling bumps, which were found on some early Spitfire IXs and were similar to those found on the Messerschmitt 109G. The* Skychief *was a conversion of a Mark V.* – R.H. Beall

Thomas Todd in AU-F of 421 Squadron. Todd is wearing his American goggles, a gift from an apologetic B-17 gunner whose aircraft Todd escorted to safety, despite the fact that it had mistakenly fired at him. Todd recalls that the goggles were very comfortable, and he used them for quite a while.

– Len Thorne

THE SKYCHIEF II

Richard "Hap" Beall, 421 Squadron

I had flown the Mark V Spitfire in 416 Squadron under Kelly Walker. He was my C.O. when I first got to the 416 in Digby. I was just beginning to get the hang of air combat under Kelly when Freddie Greene took over, and I happened to be transferred to 421 Squadron.

In the 421 we also flew the Mark V, but in the middle of 1943 we began to receive the newer Mark IX. Since we only had a few of them to start with, we had to take turns flying them. Red Omand, who was senior to me, had first dibs on the *Skychief II* (AU-G, BR 138). The name matched the "Red Indian" crest of 421 Squadron very well.

My memory of the *Skychief II* is that it was far superior to the old Mark Vs. I was a bit wary of it at first. On June 9, 1943, while I was practice flying it, my No. 1, Joe MacFarlane (EN 180), collided with Bill Sherlock (BS 306). Joe bailed out OK and Bill managed to belly-land his aircraft back at base, with only about two-thirds of his port wing.

A few days later, in the *Skychief II,* I was going over the Channel to Tricqueville and trying to catch up with the squadron—full throttle—when the supercharger kicked in. I thought I had been hit, or collided with someone myself. It was quite a blast.

Nevertheless, our Ramrod was successful. We saw a few Me 109s around and saw one get shot down by a 403 pilot. We made a lot of contrails around 33,000 feet. It was a pleasure to fly a Mark IX and know you had a superior aircraft. Johnnie Johnson was our wing commander at the time, and you can't get better than that. So we had a lot of confidence—in the leadership we had and in the aircraft we flew. The squadron still had Mark Vb's, which flew in mixed formations with Mark IXs and were used for air-to-air firing practice and so on.

Later on, in 1945, for my second tour, I had my own aircraft, AU-H (SM 309), with *Panama Bound* in white lettering on the nose since I was from the Panama Canal Zone.

"Red" Omand was the usual pilot of the Skychief II *along with Richard Beall in 1943.* – R.H. Beall

The ground crew of the Skychief II *1943.* – R.H. Beall

Pilots of 421 Squadron, 127 Wing, Kent, England, in August 1943.
Front row: F/O Isbister, F/L Roger Wilson, F/O Johnny Drope, F/O Musgrave, F/L Wally Quint, F/O Gord Driver, F/S Warfield, F/O Wilson, F/L Patterson.
Second row: P/O Jack Banford, F/O Webb Harten, F/S Len Thorne, F/L Dagwood Philips, S/L Buck McNair, D.F.C. with two bars, W/C J.E. Johnson, D.F.C. with bar, F/L Norman Fowlow, F/O "Red" Omand, F/O Hank Zary, F/O Nickerson.
Back row: P/O Dixon, F/O Cook, P/O Carl Linton, F/O Johnny Hicks, F/O Paul Johnston, F/O Tommy Parks, F/O Al Flemming, F/L J. "Tiger" Sherlock, F/O McLaughlin, F/O Packard, F/O Denancrede. – Len Thorne

Gord Driver, 421 Squadron, with a Spitfire IX, AU-L (MA 232), early in 1944. – Len Thorne

RAMROD 133: MY FIRST MISSION

Len Thorne, 421 Squadron

IT was my first operational trip. We were briefed to escort 240 Fortresses that were set to bomb the airfield at Paris. The C.O. of 421 Squadron was S/L Buck McNair, D.F.C. I flew No. 2 to F/L Art Sager in Green Section. It was July 14, 1943.

Our squadron flew in three sections, with four aircraft in line astern. We took off at seven in the morning and climbed steadily to 26,000 feet to meet the Forts.

The 403, commanded by S/L Hugh Godefroy, always flew with 421, taking turns—one as top cover, the other as bottom cover.

The sky was cloudless and you could see for miles. This being my first do, I was sticking pretty close to my No. 1. Some Me 109s were spotted at nine o'clock to us in the sun, but try as I did, I couldn't see them. The Huns scooted by and we continued on with the Forts.

Then my auxiliary tank ran dry and the engine cut! That shook me to the teeth, and I sat there waiting for it to catch again after I'd switched to my regular tank. It finally caught, but I had to go through the gate to catch up!

Some more 109s tried to bounce the Forts again 10 miles southeast of Evreux. I saw one Fort burning with one hell of a fire. A 109 exploded in midair as the Forts bagged him.

When we were on the other side of Evreux, we could make out Paris. We had penetrated as far as we dared and had to let the Forts continue while we started for home.

All the flying on this trip had been done between 26,000 and 32,000 feet. I didn't have any gloves, and my fingers damn near froze. Just two years before, I had won my wings— two years to my first show!

A Spitfire IX, (BS 147), possibly coded AU-U. The pilot in the cockpit is Len Thorne, 421 Squadron. January 1944. Note the dual badges of the 421—the McColl-Frontenac Oil Company Indian decal, and the Maple Leaf in the style used by 403 Squadron. – Len Thorne

Pilots of 403 Squadron, March 23, 1943
Left to right: Sgt. Chevers, F/O Wozniak, F/L Godefroy, F/O Fowlow, Sgt. Deschamps, P/O Lane, P/O Dowding, F/O Aitken, F/L Magwood, F/O Brannagan, F/L Richer, Padre (name unknown), Sgt. Cottrill, Sgt. Uttley, P/O Dover, Sgt. Miller, Sgt. Hamilton, Sgt. Brown. – Roy Wozniak

This Spitfire IX, KH-A (LZ 997), was regularly flown by F/L Wally Conrad of 403 Squadron. On August 17, 1943, he flew over France in Ramrod 206, Part Two. During an attack on a German FW 190, F/S G.M. Shouldice (MA 615) collided with Conrad's aircraft, tearing the tail unit and aileron completely off. Miraculously, Conrad survived a very low-altitude jump without time for his parachute to fully deploy. He fell into a haystack and was rescued by the French resistance. He walked over the mountains to Spain, returned to England, and became the commander of 421 Squadron. Shouldice was less fortunate. He tried to nurse his damaged Spitfire back across the Channel. He could not bail out because his canopy was damaged, and his aircraft plunged into the Channel.
– DND RE68-1155, Steve Sauvé

Ramrod to Mondidier

Norm Chevers, 403 Squadron

I flew in 403 Wolf Squadron, RCAF. It was considered a very hot squadron.

On October 24, 1943, we were on a ramrod to Mondidier aerodrome. My logbook says, "Bags of hun." I was flying a Spitfire IX (KH-L, MH 840) as No. 2 to the wing commander, Hugh Godefroy, who was flying HCG (MH 831). Wing commanders had their initials painted on the side of their aircraft.

Halfway through the mission, Godefroy's aircraft wasn't acting right. He figured he wouldn't be much use in a dogfight, so I was escorting him out.

The squadron was bounced by 20 FW 190s. Godefroy and I got lost from the squadron. We had quite a number of 190s after us. We continued to climb and got into some very high cirrus cloud, but we were still being pursued. We were at maximum power, and Godefroy kept asking me, "Number Two, where are you?" and I answered, "Right up your chuff, right up your chuff!" You could see the German planes—they kept trying to catch us, and they were firing away like hell, but they were going astray because we were turning inside them and climbing at the same time. That was the best feature in the Spitfire—a very tight, climbing turn. We evaded them quite well that way, because they couldn't turn within our radius—they kept flicking off into spins.

The rest of the squadron had a hell of a time getting out of France. It was quite a Donnybrook. We lost the flight commander, F/L Southwood (MH 665). J.D. Browne (MA 578) got one destroyed, and one damaged, and the 403's C.O., R.A. Buckham, well, he came back with a

F/L Hugh Godefroy in May 1943, with his Spitfire IX, KH-F (EN 130), painted to show his three victories. – N. Ogilvie

cannon shell in his engine. Fortunately his aircraft still worked but it was losing power all the way (MH 835).

As I said, in the Spitfire we could outclimb the 109. We could climb up to 30,000 feet, if necessary, to get away. The superchargers would cut in between 20,000 and 21,000 feet. The Germans couldn't manoeuvre as well, and many times that's what did them in.

In the Spitfire, we always had a way out. Knowing we could get away from them in a tight, climbing turn gave us a lot of confidence. However, for that day my logbook says, "I'm still shaking!"

P/O Norm Chevers of 403 Squadron, 1943. – Norm Chevers

"Buzz" Beurling's Spitfire IX, VZ-B (MH 883), 412 Squadron, between December 1943 and February 1944. The 30 small swastikas along the nose mark the victories Beurling had scored up to that time. – Cecil Brown, Beurling Family

My System

George "Buzz" Beurling, D.S.O., D.F.C., D.F.M., 403, 412 Squadrons

EVER since I was a kid, I've been nuts about flying. In fact, come to think of it, flying is about all I've ever been interested in.

People keep asking me what my system is. There's nothing particularly complicated about it. It's a matter of training your eyes to focus swiftly on any small object that's out there.

First comes shooting. I became interested in shooting and I spent a lot of time practising, especially working on deflection shooting against moving targets.

Here's the way it works: I try to shoot at 300 yards, because that is the range my cannon is harmonized for. But often, I can't work it that fine, and that's where deflection shooting and a lot of just plain shooting comes in.

You see, if the target gets inside that 300 yards, you are shooting two streams of stuff at it. I have figured out how far those streams are apart, and I try to get one stream hitting the target, forgetting the other. That means I actually have to aim at something else to make my hit. So, I take a line off an exhaust or something else handy, allow for the speed I am travelling and the speed the enemy is travelling, and then let go. It sounds complicated, but it isn't too hard. In fact, it's really quite simple. I don't think some of the fellows apply themselves to it enough.

I like to get above the enemy planes if possible. You see, they came in on Malta that way—a wave of bombers, then a couple of waves of fighters, usually high above them. If I can get up above the fighters, I come down in a power dive, probably reaching 600 miles an hour. I go right through the fighter wave.

I always try for two fighters in a big formation and it's not too hard to do it, if it's done right. By that time I'm through to the bombers. My speed should have carried me free of the fighters for a short spell at least. It usually should be a cinch to get a bomber.

I never attack from dead astern, and most of the time the way I fight depends on deflection

George "Buzz" Beurling of 403 Squadron, September 1943. – Len Thorne

shooting. I practise that as long and as often as I can, and I'll keep on practising as long as I fly.

I think this is of the utmost importance because the longer I fly, and the more operations I see, the more I'm convinced that in this racket, it's the man who spots the other man first who comes out on top in the end. Given good eyesight, and lots of practice, there's no reason why any pilot shouldn't be able to train himself to do this.

You have to profit by your mistakes, too. I know I've made lots of mistakes, but I like to think I only made the same ones once. When I know I've made a mistake, I try to figure out the reason for it, and make sure it doesn't happen again.

From a 1943 interview with Canada's top ace by J.R. Keith in Air-Age *magazine.*

This Spitfire V, YO-A (EN 921), with a painting of a lady on the cowling, was the aircraft of F/O Jack Sheppard of 401 Squadron, Biggin Hill. October 15, 1943. – DND PL 22146

We Bagged a 109 a Minute

Lloyd Chadburn, D.S.O., D.F.C., 402, 416 Squadron

OUR luck was in the day we got the ten Jerries. Not that it was all luck, of course. My boys are good and the Hun just doesn't seem to have the guts for a fight. Why, one of them bailed out of his aircraft before we had even hit him. [November 3, 1943, Ramrod 290. Available records show Chadburn was flying his personal Spit V, coded with his initials LVC, EP 548.]

But I'm getting ahead of myself. When I was asked to write this piece, I was told to just dish up the facts as they come, to give a sort of play-by-play description. I was told, "Tell it in your own language, and if people don't always understand what you say, they'll at least get a picture of what an air battle is like."

All I can say is that an air fight is a pretty complicated business. It takes just a few minutes for a heck of a lot to happen, and I'm not sure I can make it come to life. But here goes.

My two squadrons (402 and 416), took off from a British aerodrome and pushed out over the North Sea to keep a rendezvous with 72 USAAF Marauders, out to prang an enemy objective [Schiphol airfield]. We found the bomber boys all right, and moved on to our objective, with nothing to hinder us but a spot of light flak along the Dutch coast.

As we turned up to the target, the flak got kind of heavy. We fighter pilots admire the bomber crews a lot. They've got to be cool as

T.K. "Ibby" Ibbotson, the usual pilot of YO-Q (W3834), Redhill, July 1943.   – Noel Ogilvie

Spitfire V, LVC (EP 548), November 1943. W/C Lloyd Chadburn flew this aircraft. He was at first refused entry into the RCAF. He persisted and became an ace, with five official victories. Through his outstanding combat leadership, his pilots also scored many victories. – RCAF

A Spitfire V (W3834), with clipped wings, from the Corps of Imperial Frontiersmen, Redhill, July 9, 1943. – DND PL 19315

blazes and they really haven't got the same chance we've got.

This time they got right on the target, pranged it according to schedule, and we all started for home. Escort methods vary, so I'm not giving away any secrets when I say that 402 Squadron, the one I was leading—that's 12 fighters—was covering a box of 36 U.S. bombers. My other squadron (416) was further back, covering a box of 18, while the box ahead of me was being looked after by some RAF boys.

Heavy flak in the target area had spread the boxes out a bit. A fighter squadron's main job is to escort the bombers. We're not supposed to run off and leave them at the first sight of an enemy aircraft. However much we may want to mix it, we've got to consider the bombers' safety first.

So the boxes were spread out. My 12 Spits were on the job. Suddenly, just as we crossed the Dutch coast, we saw between 14 and 18 Me 109s following the box of 18 bombers ahead. I think the Jerries thought they were having a go at the last box in the line, not realizing we were also in Holland.

I guess we were about five miles off the coast with the 109s about four miles ahead, when I ordered my section to start moving out. A squadron flies in three sections of four aircraft each, so if we spread out enough we have a better chance of pocketing the Jerries, who usually won't fight if they can get out of it.

Seconds later, S/L G.E.W. Northcott of Minedosa, Manitoba (EP 120), leading B Flight, attacked two 109s that were slightly above him and almost head on. He climbed up into them. They dove straight down, moving too fast for him to close with them. By this time, F/L D.R. Mitchener, D.F.C., of Saskatoon (BM 211), and I were moving into them. Mitch engaged one. The Hun did a few steep turns, got frightened, and jumped out. He was yellow. Score one.

I engaged the other aircraft. I fired. The Hun caught fire and hit the sea. Score two.

Geoff Northcott, who had been unable to engage the two he'd driven our way, came over and gave us a hand. On the way, he saw two Jerries and moved in to attack. Just as he got in a short burst at one of them, F/O Dodd, D.F.C.

S/L Geoff Northcott 402 Squadron, with his Spitfire V, AE-A (EP 120), showing nine victories. November 1943. This aircraft is now in the IWM Fighter Collection, Duxford, England. – Rick Richards

(EP 445), in Geoff's No. 3 position, came up and said on the R.T., "Graham's been shot down, Geoff!"

Geoff looked back, saw an aircraft on fire, and figured Dodd was right. Actually, it turned out to be the Hun fighter Geoff had shot at himself. The Jerry crashed in the drink. Score three.

I know this seems mixed up and confusing, but it gives a good idea of the strange mistakes pilots can make while moving through three dimensions at high speeds. Graham had been flying beside Geoff, and what Dodd actually saw take fire was the Hun Geoff had just pranged. So you see that it's quite possible to score against an enemy, take your eyes off him for a moment, then look back and think it another guy in trouble.

Incidentally, Graham (BM 535) got lost in this mix-up, and, unable to rejoin his squadron, did the right thing and beat it for home. A lone aircraft is duck soup for two or more enemy fighters.

While all of this was happening, Mitchener and I were polishing off our first Jerries. Then Mitch lit into another 109 and, since he seemed by himself, I decided to give him cover. Mitch was racing around like a dingbat. I said, "Keep after him, Mitch, I've got you covered." Mitch closed in fast and I could see him getting cannon strikes on the enemy's fuselage. The Jerry caught fire. The pilot bailed out. Score four.

Next thing I noticed was a dogfight off to the north of me. I turned toward it, and saw a Spitfire chasing a 109, with another 109 on our chap's tail. I broke into the Jerry following our man, fired a couple of bursts from 300 yards, and swung over the top of him. He burst into flames and hit the deck. Those 109s catch fire quicker than almost any other type of fighter. Score five.

So much for the squadron I was leading—City of Winnipeg (402). The total score from Wing was ten, so we'll have to see what the City of Oshawa (416) Squadron was doing, under S/L Freddie Green, D.F.C. (EP 452).

They had been escorting the last box of Marauders, and just as they crossed the Dutch coast, F/L Art Sager of Vancouver (BM 471) dived to attack four Messerschmitts that were attempting to break up the American bomber formation. Two Jerries broke to the port of the bombers, and two to starboard. Sager and his No. 2 went after the Huns, who broke to the right. He let go a quick burst to make them turn so he could close in. At about 300 yards, Sager saw black smoke pouring from the Hun. He saw him crash. Score six.

Sager then went after the other 109 and got some hits, but had temporary gun stoppages, so F/L D.E. Noonan of Kingston (AB 234) took over. He closed in to about 200 yards, saw strikes on the enemy's fuselage, and saw him crash. The Jerry is shared between Sager and Noonan. Score seven.

Meanwhile, P/O W.H. Jacobs (BL 430) lit into a 109. It was seen to crash on the outskirts of the Dutch town of Zandervoort. Score eight. [Flying Officer Jacobs was reported missing on this mission.]

After helping Sager finish off the Jerry, Noonan, who had gone right down on the deck after it, climbed to 2,000 feet to escape flak. Up the coast, he saw a lone 109 approaching from the west. The Hun attempted to outmanoeuvre, but Noonan blew his cockpit off and raked him along the fuselage. Jerry flicked over and dived vertically for the deck. Art Sager saw the 109 crash in Zandervoort's main street. It went ploughing up against a storefront. A big day for Zandervoort. Score nine.

F/L R.D. Booth of Vancouver (AR 383), leading another section of the Oshawa squadron, spotted three enemy aircraft. He dived under his section, broke on the last Hun, and opened fire. The enemy rolled down to 1,000 feet with Booth on his tail. Suddenly, the 109 flicked on its back and went into the deck. Score ten.

There they are. Ten victories. The time was about ten minutes. But one thing should be clearly understood. Our main job is to escort bombers on the way into the target. We don't fight unless we have to. But the target had been pranged, so we decided to have a go. And, believe me, what a go it was!

From The Star Weekly, *Toronto,*
December 31, 1943.

Rhubarb Over Holland

Art Sager, D.F.C., 416 and 443 Squadrons

It happened on November 13, 1943. We were stationed at Digby in Lincolnshire under the inspiring leadership of Lloyd Chadburn, D.S.O., D.F.C. Ebullient Freddie Green was C.O. of 416 and I was a flight commander. We were escorting bombers south over France and east over Holland but were frequently grounded or recalled because of bad weather.

We were restless, wanting more action. I got the idea of doing a rhubarb over the Zuider Zee, the inland sea north of Amsterdam. Intelligence had reported that German torpedo bombers—which had been attacking our coastal shipping—were training in this area. My plan was to take three other pilots, all volunteers, and fly across the North Sea at wavetop level. We would hit the coast at a lightly defended spot, streak across the 25 miles of flat farmland to the Zuider Zee, and look for German bombers on practice runs.

As I learned later, during a visit to Holland after the war, there were no "lightly defended" areas along this coastline: the Germans, preparing for a possible invasion, had constructed a continuous line of fortifications and gun placements from the Hoek to Den Helder. Had I known this at the time I doubt that I would have proposed such a mission, as the risks were far too high.

The cloud level was low and it was raining that morning. Met predicted the same across the North Sea, with a 10-mile wind from the northwest. This was ideal weather for a rhubarb.

All the flight had volunteered, and I picked Noonan (DN-W, EP 452), Dubnick (DN-Y, EP 564), and Gould (DN-O, AB 910), all good,

Art Sager with his Spitfire V, DN-P (EN 950), November 13, 1943. – I.W.M., CH 110

The Spitfire XVI of 443 Squadron's C.O., S/L Art Sager, 21-D, Ladykiller *(TB 476), in April 1945.* – Art Sager

experienced pilots. Danny Noonan was my No. 3, second in command. We flew at cruising speed, 40 feet above the waveless water. You had to keep your eyes on the altimeter as cloud and sea meshed together. I was steering a compass course for 10 miles north of IJmuiden, where, Intelligence had said, there were no anti-aircraft guns. From there we'd head for Edam on the Zuider Zee.

After we'd been flying about 30 minutes, the cloud base rose, but I decided it was safe enough to continue. When the Dutch coast appeared as a thin line on the horizon, I checked the profile map I'd strapped to my knee and saw that we were south of our landfall: the line of buildings directly ahead coincided with those of IJmuiden. I turned 10 degrees port for one minute, got back on course, and then waggled my wings. This was the signal to drop our extra fuel tanks.

Heading now for a seemingly uninhabited point on the coast, I pushed the throttle steadily ahead up to the gate, and the four of us, 50 yards apart lined abreast, crossed a sandy beach very low and very fast.

We were crossing sand dunes when there was an explosion. I must have been momentarily concussed, as I was thrown forward over the stick. When I opened my eyes through the smoke all I saw were red lights on the instrument panel. Expecting a fire, I sat up, pulled the stick back, and reached for the canopy hood, getting ready to bail out. But in seconds the smoke cleared. And my hearing returned: I could hear the blessed roar of the Merlin. I dropped down to the level of the scrub trees and switched on the radio to ask if the others were OK. For some reason all of them were flying very close.

The radio wasn't working and I saw that most of the instruments were out as well. Realizing that I could no longer lead, I hand-signalled Danny to take over and continue. Not knowing how badly I'd been hit, I decided I'd best head for home, as I'd be a drag on the others. I turned 180 degrees, and when I looked around the other three were with me, Danny up front, leading. They'd seen the hole in my kite and weren't sure I'd make it.

I might not have, either, as I had no air speed indicator or altimeter and the compass was wavering erratically. I was delighted to have their company and very pleased later to be on the ground.

It was a 20 mm shell that caught me, just behind the armour plating. It exploded inside and came out like shrapnel. There were pieces of metal in the cockpit and I was very lucky not to have been a recipient of one of them. It was a miracle that the control cables were not cut.

A Belly Landing

Sten Lundberg, 416 Squadron

ON May 21, 1944, we were cruising at treetop level between trains, hiding behind any and all terrain to avoid being seen. This was the practice till we should see smoke on the horizon from the next train along the track we were following. Our speed was about 340 miles an hour.

Someone on the ground, manning a 20 mm A.A. gun, put a round into my Spitfire (DN-T) as I crossed his position. I smelled the cordite and, of course, heard the impact, but I could see no damage nor did anything seem wrong with my aircraft.

I told my flight commander, Forbes-Roberts, that I had been hit and presented the bottom of my aircraft to his view. He could see nothing wrong. About three minutes later, after pulling up from an attack on the next train and a water tower in a marshalling yard, the temperature gauge for the coolant started climbing and the pressure began dropping.

That's when I noticed the hole, about eight inches across and some two feet from my seat, in the starboard wing right over the cooler radiator. I proceeded to climb as white smoke billowed out from the exhaust stacks. By the time I reached 3,000 feet, flames had started coming out. That was my signal to switch off and tell the flight leader I was going to bail out.

I remember the response: "OK, Lundy—good luck!"

In my haste, I neglected to unlock the coupe top, and instead just pulled the jettison toggle. The lock jammed and, as far as I was concerned, the aircraft was on fire and I was stuck.

I hammered on the canopy in complete panic. Finally, the Spit started to shudder. This

This Spitfire IX (MH 850), of 411 Squadron, Tangmere, was usually flown by F/L G.W. Johnson. May 1944. – Ken Johnson, Clerihew

brought me to my senses, and I realized the plane was about to stall, so I shoved forward on the stick.

I pushed up on the rear of the canopy and in so doing broke the lock. The whole thing then settled in front of me like another windshield. I managed to get rid of it to the left side and fortunately it did not hit the tail.

By this time I was at only 600 feet with no engine power. To me that was too low to even consider bailing out. So I landed wheels up in a farmer's field straight ahead. Successfully, I might add. Naturally, I left the aircraft quickly when it came to rest, since I was sure it was still on fire.

I looked back at it when I was some 40 or 50 yards away. There it sat, as pretty as ever except for the prop and the belly. I moved back toward the plane with the intention of setting off the little thermite bomb that was installed in the cockpit for the purpose of burning the aircraft under just such circumstances.

I don't think I took more than three steps when I heard a whiz and bang of gunshot. This stopped me in my tracks. As I looked around, I saw ten Luftwaffe A.A. personnel around me at the edge of the field. They had obviously been watching the whole procedure. Since I had landed within 200 yards of their battery of 40 guns, which I could not see from the air because of camouflage, I quickly became a prisoner.

They thought I had bailed out. Probably some puffs of white smoke from the glycol looked like my parachute streaming.

From the time of my decision to bail out till actual touchdown was about two minutes — about as long as it takes to read this account.

416 Squadron, Tangmere, May 1944.
Front row: P/O W. Palmer, F/O Bill Simpson, F/S J.A.R. Boulais, F/O A.J. Fraser, W.O. J.E.R. McCrea, F/O J.B. Rainville, F/L D.W. Hayworth, F/O Torkelsson Lundberg, F/S J.C.R. Maranda, F/O B. Eskow, F/O R. Rosario St. Georges, P/O K. Forbes Scott.
2nd row: F/S J.C. Greeman, F/L W.F. Mason, F/L G.R. Patterson, F/O D.R. Cuthbertson, F/O G.A. Borland, F/O A.R. McFadden, F/L D.E. Noonan, S/L Green; F/L D.F. Prentice, F/L J.L. Campbell, F/O J.D. Gould, F/O D.W. Harling, G.H. Farquharson, and atop the aircraft, F/O A.J. Tafuro. – DND PL 26651, Sten Lundberg

Dogfight Over Italy

Bert Houle, D.F.C. with bar, 145, 213, 417 Squadrons

WHEN war was declared I immediately attempted to enlist in the RCAF as a fighter pilot, as that seemed to be the only option that provided individual competition in combat. I was not accepted until Friday, September 13, 1940. During elementary training at Regina I won the bracelet for leading my course in ground studies and flying the Tiger Moth. Following this, I was transferred to No. 32 SFTS at Moose Jaw, Saskatchewan, for training on Harvards. After receiving my wings I was posted overseas. I sailed on HMS *California*, and during the voyage we listened to Lord Haw-Haw brag that the *Bismarck* had sunk us.

After training at Usworth on Hurricane Is, about 60 pilots, mostly Canadian, were selected to fly long-range Hurricane IIs off the *Ark Royal* aircraft carrier to Malta. With my 178 hours total flying time, I was a little apprehensive, as it was the type of operation that had to be done right the first time.

I was posted to 213 Squadron for the defence of Cyprus, and later to Alexandria. I did not really get into combat until July 1942. We flew Hurricane IICs with the two outboard cannons removed. It did not give us much of a fire pattern and we were almost helpless against the much faster, higher-flying Me 109s. My first success came on September 1, 1942, when I was leading ten Hurries against a Ju 88 bomber raid on our El Alamein line. My cannons seized after a short burst, and as my aircraft had been hit by return fire, I turned for base. My No. 3 confirmed my kill. The squadron counted three destroyed, but we had lost five aircraft. Two pilots were killed and three walked back. I was acting flight commander at the time; the other flight commander was Jock Cameron (later Sir Neil Cameron, G.C.B., C.B.E., D.S.O., D.F.C., A.D.C., RAF, Chief of the Air Staff).

My most memorable action occurred on October 26, 1942. Just at dusk I got into two squadrons of Ju 87s flying west into an illuminated sky. I was in relative darkness. With the first three aircraft I got so close that the bullets straddled the target. Slight right rudder put the left cannon on target. On the fourth Stuka I inadvertently pushed forward on the stick, and the result was spectacular. Each cannon fired into a wing-root fuel cell, and both cells blew up. I watched mesmerized while the aircraft went into a slow spiral from about 700 feet and crashed on a sandy spit. I damaged another enemy aircraft, then throttled back and headed for home. I was awarded the D.F.C. for this action.

After the El Alamein line broke, 213 and 238 Squadrons landed more than 100 miles behind enemy lines and strafed the roads used by the enemy. We were moved out on the third day after wiping out two armoured columns that had moved within 30 miles of us on a desert track that led to the Gialo oasis. We had flown into this landing ground on Friday, November 13. I shared a Fieseler Storch in the air but have never included it in my score as I was ashamed to claim an unarmed opponent. I also destroyed at least one and probably two Savois SM 79s on the ground.

When W/C Darwin took over the Spitfire wing in November 1942, he took me with him as a flight commander in 145 Squadron. I shot down an Me 109 before going off for a rest in January 1943. A review of the fortunes of those officers with me at that time indicates just how dangerous war can be. W/C Darwin was later killed in Italy. His replacement, W/C Ian Gleed, was killed before the fall of Tunis. His replacement, W/C Olver, was shot down over Sicily and went P.O.W. My C.O., Roy Marples, was killed in England, and his replacement, Lance Wade, was killed in Italy. The other flight commander, John Taylor, was killed in Sicily.

In June 1943 my posting came through as flight commander of 417 Squadron. It was located at Ben Cardane in Algeria. Most of the personnel and equipment were on ships, and we were not to meet up with them until we landed

S/L Bert Houle, 417 Squadron, with his Spitfire VIII, AN-A (JF 457). Note the hole in the mirror made by a 20 mm shell during combat with German FW 190s on January 22, 1944. – DND RE74-216

in Sicily. There was little action there. S/L Stan Turner and I were blown up on a Jerry land mine while seeking an HQ for A.V.M. Broadhurst. Both my eardrums were punctured, and I was grounded on doctor's orders for a month. I got back flying just as we were being reequipped with new Spitfire VIIIs and preparing to fly into Italy—the first full-scale invasion of the mainland of Europe in the Second World War. A promotion to S/L gave me command of the 417. About that time, on October 4, 1944, in AN-M (JF 469), I shot down three enemy fighters over the east coast of Italy toward Termoli. My No. 2 claims I got two FW 190s in 15 seconds.

In mid-January, we were moved to the west coast to cover the Anzio beachhead. I was credited with the first enemy fighter (a 190) shot down over the beachhead on the first morning of the invasion, January 22, 1944. My own aircraft (AN-A, JF 457, my usual aircraft) was badly shot up, and one photo shows me poking my finger through the hole in the mirror that was made by a 20 mm bullet while I was attacking a second 190. On January 27, I added an Me 109 destroyed and one damaged (AN-A, JF 936). I added another destroyed on February 7 near Lake Bracciaogno, north of Rome (AN-E, JG 173).

In my last dogfight, on February 15, 1944 (AN-A, JG 184), the squadron claimed six FW 190s destroyed. After assessing the camera gun films, our wing commander awarded two to me, but I gave one up to be credited to three of the other pilots. In that action, I was hit by a slug that lodged along my carotid artery. I was awarded a bar for my D.F.C., and received both decorations from George VI at an investiture in Buckingham Palace on April 18, 1944. I was then repatriated to Canada, and denied another tour, mainly because the press declared that two tours were enough.

My favourite fighter was the Spitfire VIII with clipped wings. It had power and good armament. It could roll quickly and out-turn any enemy fighter we encountered. My proudest boast is that I never had a pilot killed in any formation of Spitfires I ever led, and that includes more than one complete tour of operations.

Dogfight Over Anzio

J.J. Doyle, D.F.C., 417 Squadron

On March 29, 1944, 417 Squadron took off from Marcianese to patrol the Anzio beachhead. I was leading Blue Section, F/L "Topsy" Turvey led Red Section. I was flying AN-R, JG 240.

We arrived on patrol, and our controller reported that 20 enemy aircraft were coming into the beachhead from the northeast. Both Red and Blue Sections saw the Me 109s and FW 190s crossing the coast to the north of Anzio. When they turned south to dive on Anzio, we turned to engage them. Topsy's section took on the top cover, and my section took on the others.

I picked a 109 passing in front of me at about 175 yards, laid on deflection, and gave him a three-second burst. I could see strikes, he started to belch out a lot of black smoke, and down he went. People on the ground confirmed the crash.

I had begun to attack a 190 when I was attacked by another, who set me afire. My No. 2, Cam Everett, took him off my hands. The fire went out, and I continued after my enemy through some flak. Through it all, I was hit four times and wounded in the back, right shoulder, head and face, and right side and leg.

Regardless, I continued to chase the 190, firing burst after burst into him. I saw strikes and black smoke coming from him before my ammo ran out. My gun camera indicated he was probably destroyed.

My engine was running rough, and I was out of ammo, so I headed for the airstrip at Nettuno. As I descended for a forced landing, the engine quit! I landed very quickly. The fuselage, which had been hit behind my armour plate, right behind my head, broke off, and I skidded to a stop.

As I was being loaded into an ambulance, the American engineering officer who was in charge of the airstrip thanked me profusely for not landing on the PSP (perforated steel planking) and messing up his runway. As if I had any desire to! With my wheels up, I would have wrapped myself up in it.

Spitfire VIII of 417 Squadron, January 22, 1944. – RCAF, Chuck Doodson

Shot Down!

Ralph Nickerson, 421 Squadron

I was shot down on May 21, 1944, while flying on Ramrod 905 with RCAF Squadron 421 out of Tangmere, England. My aircraft was a Spitfire IXb (AU-D, MJ 928).

Our fighter wing moved from Kenley to Tangmere in April 1944. There we joined a large number of other fighters, all lining up for D-Day.

We continued our regular operations escorting bombers over the continent to the limit of our range and going out on fighter sweeps. Sometimes the whole wing went, sometimes just four of us. If the latter, we generally took off before dawn in the hope of surprising some Jerries on the ground. However, on May 21, the entire wing was organized to take off early in the morning. Our target was literally anything that moved over parts of Belgium and France.

This was the first time in a long while that we were actually going after ground targets, and we were all looking forward to a good show. While taxiing out that morning, I had a flat tire, so was delayed a while. I caught up with our wing at Lympne, where we all landed to refuel and coordinate timing. We went in, squadron by squadron, several minutes apart and crossed into Belgium, planning to sweep south and west, over parts of France, and then return.

The gang I was with (I am not sure whether I was leading the flight or was No. 3) attacked one or more small convoys on land and one train. After half an hour or so, I discovered that I was alone with my No. 2. Not to worry.

We carried on and attacked a train, without much result. By this time our supply of petrol was getting low, so we swung west and a little north.

We were at about 3,000 feet when I spotted a field at ten o'clock that was filled with anti-aircraft guns. I swung to starboard and started down to make myself a little harder to hit, and at the same time warned my No. 2 to duck (he was about 200 yards to my starboard). As I looked back, I could see the Jerries running from their huts toward their guns. This was very surprising, as we knew that they were generally at the ready.

So we swung back to about 3,000 feet and carried on. About one minute later I discovered a twin of the anti-aircraft field almost dead ahead. Thinking about the previous field, I pushed the nose down and went in. I wanted the Jerries realize there was a war on even though it was Sunday morning about nine o'clock.

Those Jerries were waiting for us. I gave them a good splash going in and then ran out of ammo—which I don't believe affected the end result. They hit my aircraft somewhere in the tail.

I was right in on them—so close I may even have hit a gun barrel or something. I was also moving at about 400 miles an hour. For whatever reason, I could not move the aircraft up and it was trying to flick over to starboard. I needed all my strength to avoid rolling over and realized I was going in.

Normally, when you are opening the coupe top of a Spit, you are on the downward leg of coming in to land and slowing down to 160 or 180 miles an hour. Even at that speed, it may take two hands. That day, going over 400, I reached up with my one free hand and opened it.

The aircraft was hardly in my control—I was just making sure it did not flick over when I hit the ground. On the first touchdown I bounced 100 feet or more, and then I bounced again, and again. I bounced four or five times, and then I was tearing along the ground. Finally, I came to a stop. My aircraft nearly cartwheeled but then settled back.

I had switched off by then, but I could hear a sizzling like something frying. I felt myself all over, leaped out of the Spitfire on the wrong side, fell, and started to run with my parachute still strapped around my rear.

I hadn't gone far, and was wondering what the hell was wrong, when I realized my chute

Ralph Nickerson, 421 Squadron, 1944. – Len Thorne

was dragging behind me. I threw it under a hedge, and my speed increased. Our training taught us to get 10 miles from the aircraft ASAP, and I did that in one great hurry. Meanwhile, my plane literally blew up. I still think that the Jerries who got there first probably thought I was in it.

I was in very good shape in those days, and I moved very fast. Going south (my intended direction to get away from the coastline) I came across a railway track and stayed with it for about an hour until it moved too far west and seemed to be heading toward a town. There were woods nearby. I stayed on the fringe of them for a while, and then followed a narrow gravel road. I finally crawled out in the middle of a large grain field and lay down on my stomach.

My legs were cut. I had earlier emptied my Mae West and had some first-aid supplies from that. I had also cut off my flying boots (from the seams down) so I was left with what looked like a pair of heavy oxfords. The epaulets and wings from my battle dress tunic were also long gone, so I hoped I simply looked like any other young French fellow with a blue jacket and pants.

My boots had a lot of blood in them, and my body in general was aching. I emptied my boots and used some ointment to cover the cuts. I took out my silk escape maps to figure out where I was and what I was going to do about it. It was around noon and the sun was beautiful. I think I slept for an hour or so. When I awoke, and very carefully looked around, all seemed quiet. I moved out of the field and continued south along a gravel trail that was close to the woods. I kept on until it started to get dark. I felt that moving in the dark was too dangerous, so I went into the woods. With my pocket knife I cut off a few spruce bows and made a bed for sleep. It was cold and my ribs pained some, but I made it through the night.

In the morning I moved on a bit, but I was hungry. Our training had told us not to approach a crowd, but that one or two French people should be safe. There was no record of the French ever turning in an Allied flyer. I came across a farmhouse and studied it for a while from behind a hedge. An elderly man came out and went into a small outbuilding for a minute or two and then returned to the house. Smoke was coming out of the chimney, and I figured someone was having breakfast.

Included in our escape package (I got to use a lot of it) was a small booklet providing English/French phrases such as "I am an English aviator," "I am hungry," "Are you connected with the army of resistance?" and so on.

So I walked up to the door and knocked, and a moment later out came the man I had seen. When I told him who I was, he took my arm and guided me into the house, where he proceeded to hug me and kissed me on both cheeks. The lady of the house did the same.

I had one of the greatest breakfasts ever—two or three fried eggs, French black bread, milk. Wonderful. Afterward, I found out they were not connected with the resistance, so I took off, which is what our training had told us to do.

I passed several similar days: walk carefully until dusk, sleep in a barn or outside in a haymow, then breakfast and walk on. The third day out, I found an old fellow who bound up my rib cage, and did a dandy job.

About the fifth day, I walked over a rise and saw the valley of the Seine. I later discovered I was about seven miles north of the city of Rouen. I sneaked down along a gravel road, in some long grass, and took a long, hard look. For a few hours I thought I would swim over at night. But it was probably too far, about half a mile. Also, there was no telling what I might meet on the other side.

A farmhouse was nearby. I slept in a barn, and early the next morning I surveyed the house. An elderly couple lived there, so I made my usual approach.

Again, kisses and "Welcome!" Into the house I went, and down I sat with the man while his wife hustled up breakfast. While we were waiting, he produced a bottle, which I assumed was wine, because I had wine everywhere else. He poured two ounces for each of us. He intended I sip it, but I raised the cup and had a big swallow. I nearly choked to death—it was Calvados, a brandy made from Normandy apples. They hastened to give me a drink of water and figured it was a hell of a joke.

This couple had a son about my age who had been in the French Armoured Corps but had escaped capture. He did not dare live with his parents—he was about six or seven miles away. They could see I was near exhaustion, so they put me to bed. The old man cycled to his son, so when I awoke they were all there. We had a party right there with unlimited wine and Calvados. We all got to bed about 7 p.m. but were up again at 2 a.m. They had a little dory hidden somewhere, and insisted on taking me over the Seine. We parted—me carrying a large loaf of home-baked bread and a big jug of wine.

Again I was in the woods—I stayed near the river. There were Germans nearby a couple of times, so I moved very carefully. I came near a group practising with a heavy machine gun, and they saw me but paid no attention.

I believe it was on the tenth day that I walked away from the river itself, down a little gravel road with high hedges on both sides, and heard someone talking. I knew they were speaking French, so I crept up behind a hedge to look.

There were two young ladies and an elderly man. They were sitting under a sun umbrella outside a small bungalow type of cottage, drinking and having a hell of a time.

I looked over the scene for a time and then pushed through the hedge, walked over, and said I was an English aviator. Pandemonium—everyone leaped up to hug and kiss me. Keep in mind I had not shaved for four days—had not really washed up at all, so I had to look a little rough. At once I *must* have a drink—Calvados, with artificial coffee, but *good*.

My only real ID was my dog tags, which I kept around my neck always. These people were indeed connected with a resistance group. One of the ladies hopped onto a bike and about an hour and a half later came back with a young man who, it turned out, was in charge of the resistance group for the area. He looked me over good, and I realized I was virtually a captive until they could be sure of me.

It was arranged that I stay there until help could be arranged to get me to Paris, the Spanish border, and on to Madrid (the usual escape route). However, D-Day arrived, June 6, 1944, and our man in charge advised me it was too dangerous to move me at all as the Germans had every crossroad guarded.

So the resistance group leader, the elderly man, and the two young ladies agreed I should remain for the time being. The elderly man, whose name was Duboc, lived about 100 yards down the road, and he held a personal hatred for the Germans. He had fought in the First and Second World Wars, and his only son was a P.O.W. He called on me every morning and every afternoon he brought me a bottle, generally Calvados—he informed me he had a cellar full.

It was extremely dangerous to tell anyone of my presence, but after a few days a professor of languages named Itasse arrived on a bike, and he had a few books in English with him. At the time, regular schools in the country were hard to come by, and he cycled around providing tuition wherever he could. His profession gave him cover if a German stopped him and asked about the books in his basket. I read almost all of Shakespeare's plays.

I also met a French gendarme who was supposedly cooperating with the Jerries but was actually acting as an informer for the French. You could say we were a happy few in some ways, as long as we were careful about noise and loose talk.

The group leader, Marcel, saw me once a week, and we would talk about his problems. I celebrated his twenty-first birthday with him. His father, a lawyer, was a prisoner in Germany. The gendarme came about once a week and liked a drink, which he always brought with him.

There were uneasy days, of course, but eventually, one Sunday morning, after three days of shells going over our heads in both directions, the South Saskatchewan Regiment showed up outside our little gate en route back to Dieppe. I startled a few of them when I walked out of the gate with the two French mademoiselles in arm and said in English, "Any of you guys from the West?" They were walking carefully in single file—their target that day was the river, and a little village about half a mile away.

A Spitfire XI (PL 775) of 541 Squadron, Benson, resplendent in its D-Day striping. June 1944. – IWM CH 13492

Reconnaissance

M.G. "Mac" Brown, D.F.C., 400 Squadron

I flew the Mark XI Spitfire in 400 Squadron, RCAF, during one of my tours. A tour could be 100 hours of operational flying. Some of the pilots I flew with had as many as three tours already. I ended up with 287 hours on ops.

The Mark XI weighed as much as the fighter, Mark IX, which it closely resembled. Instead of guns, we had two 36-inch vertical cameras mounted in the aircraft, along with two 14-inch oblique cameras for low-level photography. We would leave our bases in England for missions as long as six hours. The aircraft had a range of 1,200 miles. Some of our missions were two to three hours to a target. During the invasion of Europe, we would sometimes fly within sight of England.

What you have to appreciate is that 400 Squadron was both a tactical and a strategic outfit. The long-range, high-altitude missions were strategic in nature, in that we were covering targets we planned to hit, or had already hit. The tactical missions tended to be short-range and low-level in support of the army. They typically lasted two to three hours.

Even on high-altitude flights, the weather could change quickly, and the target could be obscured by cloud. As we were a photographic unit, we had to bring back pictures! Otherwise, we had accomplished nothing. So in some cases, we had to come down low to take our photos. This meant fighters and more accurate flak.

Since our flights tended to be so long, a lot could happen in the course of a few hours. The weather back at base could be totally different than when we left. What had been a sunny day could become fog. We would have to land, sometimes with disastrous results.

During all this time, I never flew one particular aircraft for any length of time. I flew whatever was available and ready at the time.

The Spitfire XI had an 87-gallon main tank but also had 210-gallon wing tanks, which were gravity fed. A six-hour mission could be very tiring, but also very satisfying when we brought back the photos that were needed.

414 Squadron, Celle, Germany, 1945. The aircraft is a Spitfire XIV.
Front row: Smith, Davis, ?, MacDonald, Lawson, Hannah, Bishop, Chapman.
Back row: ?, Wetson, Pearson, Sawyer, Hall, Prendergast, Blakeney, Latch, Fuller, Appleby, Kemble, and atop the aircraft, D. Barclay. – Ken Lawson

Fighter Reconnaissance

Ken Lawson, 414 Squadron

In the European theatre, the RCAF fighter reconnaissance squadrons were attached to 39 Reconnaissance Wing. This wing was composed of three squadrons: the 400, whose aircraft were painted blue and did high-level photography; and the 414 and 430, which were known as fighter reconnaissance squadrons. These squadrons flew Mustangs and Spitfire IXs during the invasion of Europe. Later, both converted to the Spitfire XIV, which by the end of the Second World War was considered the top of the line—one of the most modern fighters in action. The Spit XIV was armed but was to be used in a defensive role only. Each fighter reconnaissance aircraft had a camera mounted just behind the cockpit that could be operated by a control on the throttle quadrant.

The reconnaissance squadrons were considered the eyes of the army and were used on a daily basis for area searches to identify enemy troop movements, concentrations, and so on. We also carried out low-level photography of rivers and surrounding areas prior to assaults or crossings. These pictures provided detailed, accurate information on heavily defended sections of proposed crossing areas. On occasion, fighter reconnaissance pilots were asked to direct the heavy artillery to targets far behind enemy lines.

These squadrons, as you can imagine, were highly vulnerable to enemy action. Heavy, medium, and light flak were usually encountered on all sorties. It could be especially disconcerting when we were flying low and on a steady course and altitude—for example, while photographing a river for an imminent crossing. Likewise, the enemy did not take kindly to aircraft directing shells onto it.

As I mentioned, the aircraft were armed but the armament was to be used only as a protective measure, since our job was not to hunt the enemy but to report on its movements so that a concentrated assault could be made by rocket- or bomb-carrying Typhoons. Even so, the fact

F/L Ken Lawson of 414 Squadron, with his Spitfire IX (FR), coded S, (MJ 351), named Violet-Dorothy *for his mother and for his wife, 1945.* – Ken Lawson

that 414 Squadron alone was credited with 28 1/2 kills suggests how important the enemy considered fighter reconnaissance pilots.

As mentioned, our daily activities were divided into area searches, photographic surveillance, and artillery shoots. Each of these missions was given a code name and was carried out by two pilots. The No. 1 pilot was

G. Wonnacott, C.O. of 414 Squadron, in front of his Spitfire IX, Q (MK 202). – Ken Lawson

briefed by an officer of the wing's Intelligence Department about his mission and was thoroughly interrogated on his return. It was the No. 2 pilot's job to keep a careful eye peeled for enemy fighters and artillery fire, and to protect the No. 1 pilot if necessary. On joining a squadron, pilots flew No. 2 for a few sorties before being promoted to No. 1. After some experience, a fighter reconnaissance pilot could be assigned either position, since the jobs were equally important. When it was imperative that information be gathered, the very experienced pilots were usually assigned. Fighter reconnaissance pilots were trained not only in fighter tactics but also as expert map readers. It was imperative that their sightings be pinpointed accurately so that appropriate action could be taken, whether that meant "calling out the Typhoons" or avoiding the area.

A fighter reconnaissance pilot might fly two or three 90-minute sorties daily, taking off by flare path at six in the morning and returning as late as nine in the evening.

During rapid advances by our armies, such as the Ardennes breakthrough, fighter reconnaissance pilots were assigned, temporarily, to the army as liaison officers. They advanced with the army in armoured cars complete with very sensitive high-powered radio equipment. Their job, under these conditions, was to work very closely with the intelligence staff of the army groups to which they were attached and to provide them with the information they requested. To this end, fighter reconnaissance sorties were assigned to general areas on a predetermined schedule. The pilot liaison officer would then call up the pilot of the aircraft on his radio and assign him a specific sortie. The pilot would radio back the information, thus providing immediate first-hand intelligence about the area ahead.

During part of the sweep through Germany, the army was concerned that, in spite of all vehicle bridges being knocked out, enemy equipment and troops still seemed to be exiting the area. I was given the mission to look at the area. It was true that all vehicle bridges had been knocked out. However, a railway bridge was still standing. I suspected that the enemy was using this bridge to move transports, troops, and so on. I took a picture of the bridge which showed that my suspicions were correct: planking had been laid across the rails, and a road access to the bridge had been constructed. Needless to say, by the next day the bridge was destroyed.

Another interesting part of my sorties involved flying over a prisoner-of-war camp that held our prisoners. I had come across it by accident one day. After circling and flying at low level across the camp, I was pleased to learn how happy the prisoners were to see one of their own planes. Whenever possible, I detoured to the camp on my way home from a sortie. After the war was over, I happened to come in touch with a couple of ex prisoners of war who remembered "that" Spitfire.

RECON OVER GERMANY

Warren Middleton, D.F.C., 430 Squadron

To many of us, war was a game of fear, bravery, and companionship. At times we had fun. It was just as easy to laugh as it was to cry. You grew up in a hurry. When speaking to other Spitfire pilots after the war, I was surprised to learn that many had never heard of 430 or 414 Squadrons, both of which were attached to 39 Recce Wing, along with 400 Squadron. Many were aware of the 400 from its early operational history overseas. As for the 430 and 414, they flew many missions over France starting in 1943 and right till the end of the war. The three squadrons were in the same wing; however, their roles were vastly different.

The 400 was a photographic reconnaissance squadron that flew Spit XIs, which were capable of flying 30,000 feet plus and had an endurance of four to five hours. Until the Germans introduced the Me 163 and Me 262, the Spit XI flew beyond the operational reach of enemy fighters. (The FW 190 could sometimes bounce Mark XIs on their climb to altitude and A.A. fire was always a threat.) I doubt that anyone in the 414 or 430 envied the pilots of the 400. Imagine being strapped in a Spitfire for five hours, freezing your tail, having to stay alert while at the same time doing pinpoint navigation and precision flying. I have seen pilots who had to be lifted out of the cockpit by the ground crew after a mission.

The 414 and 430 Squadrons did tactical reconnaissance armed with 50-calibre machine guns and 20 mm cannon. In addition, each aircraft had an oblique-facing camera mounted behind the pilot's seat in the fuselage. A more appropriate term would have been "fighter recce squadrons."

For special low-level missions, the aircraft had three oblique cameras mounted in a 90-gallon drop tank under the belly of the aircraft. Most of our missions were between 1,600 and 2,000 feet, an altitude known to most as the light flak alley. We often felt we were flying over a tennis court, as the flak coming up looked like orange tennis balls. We flew these missions at as low a speed as possible. This saved fuel and enabled us to see better so that we could mark any enemy ground activity on our large-scale

Richard Rohmer of 430 Squadron is third from the left, with his dog. Eindhoven, the Netherlands, 1945. – William Golden, C.W.H. (Hamilton)

maps. At times, we banked the aircraft on its side and took pictures of unusual events. I was once able to record the actual firing and take-off of a V-2 rocket over Holland.

We flew these missions in pairs, with the No. 1 and No. 2 covering each other's tails, weaving back and forth and changing height to avoid flak and hoping not to be bounced by enemy or friendly aircraft. We didn't see many enemy aircraft at this low altitude, but some of us had life-and-death struggles with our USAAF friends, who were prone to attack anything that flew, with all guns blazing.

We were cleared to attack ground targets if the section leader considered the target important enough. We lost too many pilots doing ground strafing, and we had to have a damned good reason for carrying out such attacks. Our tactical information was considered to be vital in determining enemy troop movements prior to offensive action.

We were truly a group of experienced pilots; I doubt that any pilot in the squadron had less than a 1,000 hours of flying time. However, many of us were hit by light flak and some didn't make it home. When you are shot at on a continuous basis for an hour at a time, experience has little to do with whether you get hit or not.

Our low-level missions using the oblique-facing cameras in the 90-gallon drop tanks were unique and memorable. I had two such missions that I will long remember: one flying from our base at Eindhoven before the Allies crossed the Rhine, and the other along the harbour at Hamburg to see if the German submarine fleet had left its concrete pens and was perhaps heading for Norway. Both missions involved flying at 150 to 200 feet in a straight line. The first covered about three miles along the Rhine River, the other covered about a mile up Hamburg's harbour. In both these missions I flew my Spit XIV with the throttle to the wall, reaching around 400 miles an hour at sea level. Fortunately, at that speed, the flak, although intense and close, passed behind us. Surprise no doubt helped — and luck.

The pictures of the Rhine were good — so I was told — and were used in the crossing of that river by the British Eighth Army. The pictures from Hamburg showed that most of the subs had left their pens. The next day, a pilot from 414 Squadron spotted at least 25 subs on the surface on their way to Norway.

A typical mission would be similar to the one I flew on April 15, 1945, in which I shot down an FW 190. My own aircraft, a Spitfire XIV, letter Y (RM 910), was being serviced, so I was assigned a backup of the same mark, letter Z (RM 824). This was my second mission of the day, and as flight commander I picked F/O Andy Anderson, a fairly new pilot in the squadron, as my No. 2. I was briefed by Intelligence to do a tactical reconnaissance in the Luneburg area. The German army was pulling back and we were to look for heavy concentrations of troops, especially armour. Air activity by the enemy had intensified in the past few days, with an attack on our base by two Me 262s with anti-personnel bombs.

No large troop movements were noted. The roads were filled with refugees and flak was light. We headed for base after about an hour, and dropped our empty fuel tanks when bogies were reported in the area. We pulled up to 5,000 feet to get out of the light flak zone and had started to breathe easy again when I spotted two fighters commencing an attack on Anderson. I called a break to starboard into the attacking fighters and tried to determine what they were. I identified the aircraft as FW 190s, and continued to turn onto the tail of the second aircraft. I opened fire at about 200 yards, only 50 rounds, and the enemy plane lost its wing and started to spin. The pilot was seen to bail out. We chased the other aircraft but it got away in some low cloud. We then returned to base. Flying time — 90 minutes.

A photo of the 430 Squadron's Spitfire XIV, letter H (RM 876), shows Al Lightbody from Montreal, an engineer by profession. He was a friend of Bill Golden, another pilot on the squadron. They were in the same OTU class.

I was flying Spitfire H (RM 876) on February 8, 1945, when I lost my No. 2, F/O Taylor, over Munich. We were attacking two FW 190s that were landing on a grass field. I hit one on the ground while he was still rolling. Taylor was hit, probably by the airfield flak, and bailed out. He waved at me but was never heard of again.

Spitfire Pilots in Hotspur Gliders

Thomas Koch, 401 Squadron

IN 1944, 401 Squadron was equipped with Hotspur gliders, which several of our pilots were sent away to learn to fly. Someone had the idea that when the invasion took place, fighters could tow gliders to France carrying ground crew and equipment.

When we finally received our Hotspurs at Biggin Hill, we had to tow them with our Spitfires instead of the Master IIs we were taught on at Netheravon. Our squadron leader, "Jeep" Neal, volunteered a not-very-happy Bill Klersey to accompany me in the Hotspur, while Sandy Halcrow piloted the Spitfire for our first tow. However, all went well and we got airborne. After releasing the tow plane, we returned safely to earth. I can't remember if Bill kissed the ground after landing, but I'm sure he was ready for a good stiff drink.

After our first tow by our Spitfire Vb's on November 23, 1943, I had four more trips in the gliders. Then, on December 15, 1943, I flew a glider with the squadron acting as escort in the Spit IXs. I can't remember whether it was the only glider being escorted or whether there were more. On January 6, 1944, the big test came—we took three gliders from Biggin Hill to Hutton Cranswick, with a lunch stop en route at Digby. Eyes must have been popping when we arrived at Digby and released our gliders from the towing Spitfires before landing. In the gliders, we had some ground crew and spare parts. With P/O Zaybeck as co-pilot, I carried the armament sergeant and parts for the tow hookup.

The Spits were refuelled and the gliders lined up alongside the runway for takeoff after lunch. A former armourer of 401 noticed the "YO" 401 letters on the aircraft and was happy to run into former acquaintances. Having a 48-hour leave pass, he asked whether he could go with us to Hutton Cranswick. Bob Hayward had extra seating in his glider, and was glad to offer him a seat.

After lunch, we took off. We were circling slowly, waiting for everyone to get off the ground when, just as Bob's glider was getting to around 500 feet, the tow rope released at the aircraft end. Bob was able to release the rope from the glider and get back to the field, where he landed safely in a crosswind. It was an excellent bit of airmanship. The glider had hardly stopped moving when its door opened and the former 401 armourer leaped out and tore across the airfield without a thank you or farewell. I wonder why.

We had to come back in as we had the hookup gear in our glider, but the exercise was still completed that day. We returned to Biggin Hill the following day, again dropping in on Digby.

In mid-February 1944, our squadron glider pilots were instructed to train pilots of 411 and 412 Squadrons, our two wing associates. For the next three weeks, our boys were busy checking out pilots of the two squadrons. Their training was as brief as possible. The first trip was a dual trip as the instructor pilot related the items to watch out for—for example, keeping the glider low on the runway to avoid tipping the tow aircraft on its nose. Trainees also learned the key altitude points and the final descent and landing.

On the second trip the pilot being trained flew the glider himself, with prompting by the instructor as required. The third trip was a solo. I can't imagine a shorter training period than that.

My last glider trip, my thirty-third, was on March 2, 1944. In all, I accumulated 175 minutes dual and 11 hours solo time. I loved the glider flights when I was taken to a higher altitude and released. Then the slipstream noise became negligible and silence prevailed. I have imagined at times how wonderful it must be in a modern soaring flyer. In these, by taking advantage of up-currents, a pilot can be airborne for hours.

A Spitfire XI, with its distinctive wing, which had no gun bulges. From 400 Squadron in early 1945.
– DND PL 43238, Steve Sauvé

400 Squadron pilots before D-Day, Odiham, England, 1944.
Front row: F/L Malcolm Brown, D.F.C., F/L Evan Tummon, S/L Paul Bissky, F/L Harold Pinsent, F/L James Stephens, F/O John Godfrey, P/O "Ben" (mascot), F/O Angus McKiggan, F/L Gus Maloney, D.F.C., F/O Ron Knewstub.
Second row: F/L Homer Walters, F/L Larry Seath, F/O John Greenwood, S/L Richard Ellis, D.F.C., F/O Wes Kennedy, F/O John Brown, F/L Art Collins, F/L Gord Brown, F/L Peter MacDonell, F/O John Henderson, F/L Art Hunter, D.F.C., F/L Alan Carlson, D.F.C.
Back row: F/L Harry Furniss, F/L Paul Wigle, F/L Joseph Morton, D.F.C., F/O Algernon Middleton, F/L Ross Matthews. – Ed Maloney, Arthur Collins

D-Day and Normandy

Larry Seath, 400 Squadron

My logbook is very brief, having only basic info as to what aircraft I flew, where to, and for how long. It's full of abbreviations and I forget some of their meanings!

All I have for D-Day is this: "June 6, 1944—Spitfire Mk. XI serial PA 900—POP—Caen area 10/10 clouds—1.25 (abortive)—'D' Day." [POP refers to "popular," a name for photo flights.]

The mind's-eye picture I have of that day has never faded, however. The cloud was at 5/10, maybe less, I could see the stream of craft heading to France, and I clearly recall the whitecaps. I was embarrassed to be going along so smoothly, as I doubted that was the case in the rough seas below.

The weather remained too cloudy for us in June. I flew again only on the 12th, 18th, and 27th, always south of Caen. Then, on July 1, 1944, we of 400 Squadron flew into airfield B8, Bayeaux. After that, we flew pretty continuously until the end of October 1944.

The thing that I remember from Bayeaux, and that I've never let myself forget, is that I have eyes that don't adjust very quickly. We were very close to the battle and on takeoff had to do a tight corkscrew climb to our operational altitude—our descent was the reverse. My depth perception had no time to adjust, hence I was waiting for the wheels to touch when I was still 20 feet in the air. Some of the others had the same problem. When this problem was realized, we were authorized to do a dummy run along the runway and via peripheral vision adjust our eyes as the trees went by. It worked like a charm. To this day, as I drive, I try to remind myself not to tailgate.

Shortly thereafter, arriving in France, we moved our Spitfires to B66 south of Diest, Belgium. We were there in a peach orchard from September 23 to October 3, 1944, when we moved to B78 Eindhoven. Our Spits were very clean looking and were unarmed.

As to the D-Day stripes on our aircraft, we had them from June 5, 1944, onwards. These stripes were applied to Allied aircraft just before D-Day so that friendly aircraft could be identified quickly. I thought we didn't need them, as we took off and rose at full bore to angel environment within the strip perimeter. Also, at height we were trying to disappear, as we were basically just a camera-equipped fuel tank, half-empty after climbing, with only our blue camouflage to protect us. So I didn't really go for the stripes, which, while they probably did some good, also made us stand out like a flag to the opposition.

To get on course for a specific photo run, we had to make a vertical-and-beyond turn on a wingtip to get over the exact start of our "on instruments" run.

Our photo section was worked off its feet after January 1944, when we started to convert from the Mustang to Spits. What with Spit practice filming to deal with, on top of operational Mustang filming till March 1944, and then operational Spit from then on, it was a very busy period.

D-Day

George Lawson, 402 Squadron

I was over on D-Day in the morning. I don't recall any combats—that is, between ourselves and other fighters—but we saw lots of action on the ground—and from our own battleships firing at us!

We still had the Mark V Spitfires at that time. We had the clipped-wing Mark Vs, and as we were training for D-Day, we were actually taking off and landing in the dark, which was a bit unusual for Spits. We were doing quite a bit of night flying so that we could handle the take-offs in the dark, be over the beachhead at dawn, stay there until dusk, and land afterward.

While training, we still flew our regular missions. On May 21, my usual aircraft, AE-H (EN 767), was hit by flak during a sweep from the Douai coast at deck level. We were shooting up trains and gun posts, according to my logbook. My "H" was washed out; even the aerial mast for the radio was shot off.

I received a new AE-H (AB 910) [now flying in the Battle of Britain Memorial Flight in Britain]. This was the aircraft I flew on June 6, 1944. It became the one I flew regularly. It was painted up with black and white stripes, and it had clipped wings. Most of the 402 Squadron aircraft had a red Maple Leaf on a white circle below the cockpit, but I don't recall any other special markings.

Later on, I flew the beautiful Mark XIV Spitfire. On October 12, 1944, according to my logbook, Bill Austin and I encountered a couple of jet-powered Me 262s. We dived on them, but they pulled away. I was flying AE-D (RM 689) [also a longtime Spitfire survivor, which flew for many years as the Rolls-Royce airshow aircraft].

In June 1944, however, we still had the Mark Vs. Not long after, we had the newer Mark IXs, and then we went on to the Mark XIVs.

Paul Day, chief pilot with the Battle of Britain Memorial Flight, meets George Lawson, pilot of Spitfire V, AE-H (AB 910), who flew in 402 Squadron on D-Day. Lawson says that the letter code H was not covered by the D-Day stripes, and that the 402 Squadron logo, "City of Winnipeg," also appeared under the windscreen. – George Lawson

D-DAY

W.A. "Art" Bishop, 401 Squadron
(son of First World War ace Billy Bishop)

I did a couple of sweeps on D-Day. Nothing much happened in the way of air combat that day, you know—we didn't really see anything. It did seem very strange to be flying over the French coast at under 1,000 feet; we were used to crossing the coast at 15,000 to 20,000, never lower, to avoid getting shot to ribbons. The weather was very poor.

On June 6, 1944, I was flying a Spitfire IX (MH 774) in 401 Squadron. We just went back and forth, back and forth, there was nothing much to it. At least we could say we had been there. The sight of all those ships was impressive. We fighter pilots were disappointed that nothing happened in the air that day—the German air force just failed to make any real opposition. The next day, of course, all hell broke loose.

On June 7 (MH 774), what actually happened was this: There was a bunch of those Ju 88s, and they dive-bombed the beach, or tried to. The first thing we saw was one hit a barrage balloon, and it just exploded—went up in a puff of smoke. Then we started chasing all the other ones, but it was kind of cloudy, and they were going in and out of the clouds. I don't think any of them came back. They never tried that again, not with those old 88 bombers.

It was all so hopeless for them. I don't know how they ever talked them into doing it, with hundreds of Allied fighters flying around. It was cloudy, and maybe they thought they could come in, drop down quickly, and go back into the clouds again. I attacked and shot down one, and well, it felt pretty good. That's what we were there for.

We were stationed at Tangmere, right on the coast. We flew straight across to the beachhead and an hour later came back. We took turns. Below, we could see the huge effort by the Navy, all those ships coming across, and the balloons bobbing around to discourage low flyers, such as the 88s. It was quite a sight.

I was not credited with any more aircraft destroyed, though I did my best. At that time, we mostly attacked ground targets. I had to drop bombs—nobody liked it, but we all had to do it. We did two weeks' training for dive-bombing. The Germans had built launching sites all over France for the V-1 weapons, called "Noballs." They were such a problem that the Allies bombed them with everything they had—heavy bombers and fighter-bombers. Anyway, we took this course in dive-bombing, and it was fine until we got over there. When you came in to attack, all this flak was flying at you. It was different from the practice runs and nobody enjoyed it much.

One day, one of the commanders from one of the other squadrons blew up just as we were going in on the target. Something hit the bomb, and it exploded, leaving just bits and pieces where there had been an airplane. So nobody really liked these missions. Still, the Germans gave up their concrete launchers and switched to mobile ones, made of metal, that they could hide in the woods and so forth. So we must have been hurting them.

Photo reconnaissance would expose these hiding places and the Allies would just bomb them and bomb them—the Forts bombed them, and the Lancs bombed them, just about everybody did. Slowing down the German "Noball" offensive was considered so urgent that we were bombing them with our Spitfires, too.

We also went after bridges. I know some people say they are hard to hit, but if you dropped a bomb in the right spot, well, that was pretty much the end of the bridge. A bridge is actually not that hard to hit—the Germans, after all, when they went into Poland at the start of the war, knocked out all the bridges in the whole country in the first couple of days. It wasn't that difficult for us, either, even if our Spitfires were not exactly designed for the job like the Germans' Stuka dive-bombers.

We didn't feel like we should be doing bombing missions. We felt like we should be looking for the Luftwaffe. The Germans had, intelligently, pulled back most of their fighters to the homeland, to fight the Forts, the American air offensive. Those few that remained weren't wasting their time on us.

I do remember one big, big fight in the middle of July 1944. It was the kind of thing you don't forget. There were just five of us who walked into this thing. We could see these planes all milling, circling around, and firing at each other, in between the cloud layers. The fight seemed to go up to 10,000 feet, with hundreds of aircraft. We climbed up above it and picked out two enemy aircraft that were still higher. We put our superchargers on, and they weren't ready for this, as they probably thought we would lose speed. As we caught up, we found that one was a Messerschmitt, while the other was a Focke-Wulf—flying together, funny thing about it.

S/L Bill Klersey knocked down the FW 190, and I went after the Me 109. I chased that son-of-a-gun down about 20,000 feet, and I couldn't catch him. I fired at him, I did everything, just sprayed him. Finally, in a break in the clouds, he levelled out, and waggled his wings at me, as if to say "screw you," and then he was gone.

Soon after that, I finished my tour and did not have a chance to get into any more air battles.

Chuck Darrow's Spitfire XVI, DN-A (TA 739), is seen here being rearmed in April 1945. – Gerry Anglin

For Serg. Magg. Falerio Gelli, 13 was an unlucky number. He became the 13th in a long list of victories gained by F/S George "Buzz" Beurling. Gelli survived this ordeal and now resides in New York State.

Keith "Skeets" Ogilvie, D.F.C., from Ottawa, flew this Spitfire I (X4107) in 609 Squadron, RAF, as his usual aircraft in September 1940.

E.N. MacDonnell flew this Spitfire II (P7856), on October 13, 1941, gaining 412 Squadron's first victory. This aircraft was also flown by J. Magee, author of the poem "High Flight," in October 1941.

S/L Jeff Northcott, D.S.O., D.F.C. with bar, from Minnedosa, Manitoba, flew this Spitfire V (EP 120) in 402 Squadron during November 1943. This aircraft is now part of the Imperial War Museum Collection, based at Duxford in England.

F/L Paul Ostrander from Winnipeg flew this Spitfire VIII (MD 280) in 155 Squadron, RAF, while stationed in Burma.

J.A. "Red" Omand and Richard "Hap" Beall flew this Spitfire IX (BR 138) in 421 Squadron during June 1943. The aircraft was originally a Mark V; it was later upgraded to Mark IX standard.

F/O P.S. Barton flew this Spitfire XI (PL 975) in 400 Squadron, on its first flight with the squadron, January 5, 1945. The aircraft's last operational flight, by F/L L.G. Aldworth, 400 Squadron, was on May 4, 1945.

F/S William G. Austin from Lakefield, Ontario, was flying this Spitfire XIV (RM 687) in 402 Squadron, on August 23, 1944, when he shot down a V-1 flying bomb.

F/L Chuck Darrow, from Toronto, flew this Spitfire XVI (TB 891) in 416 Squadron during May 1945.

W/C John Kent, D.F.C. with bar, A.F.C. with bar, C.D., from Winnipeg, flew this Spitfire V (AB 790). As Canada's first wing commander, Kent led the Polish Wing at Northolt, including 303, 306, 308, and 315 Squadrons, RAF, during 1941.

W/C Lloyd Chadburn, D.S.O. with bar, D.F.C., Croix de Guerre, Legion of Honour, from Montreal, flew this Spitfire V (EP 548) in November 1943. Lloyd was considered one of Canada's finest wing commanders.

W/C Hugh Godefroy, D.S.O., D.F.C. with bar, from Toronto, flew this Spitfire IX (MH 831) in October 1943 after taking over 127 Wing from "Johnnie" Johnson. Godefroy claimed seven victories and three damaged.

W/C "Johnnie" Johnson, C.B., C.B.E., D.F.C. with bar, D.L., from England, flew this Spitfire IX (MK 329) as a backup for his usual aircraft (MK 392) during June 1944. Note the beer keg attached to the underwing.

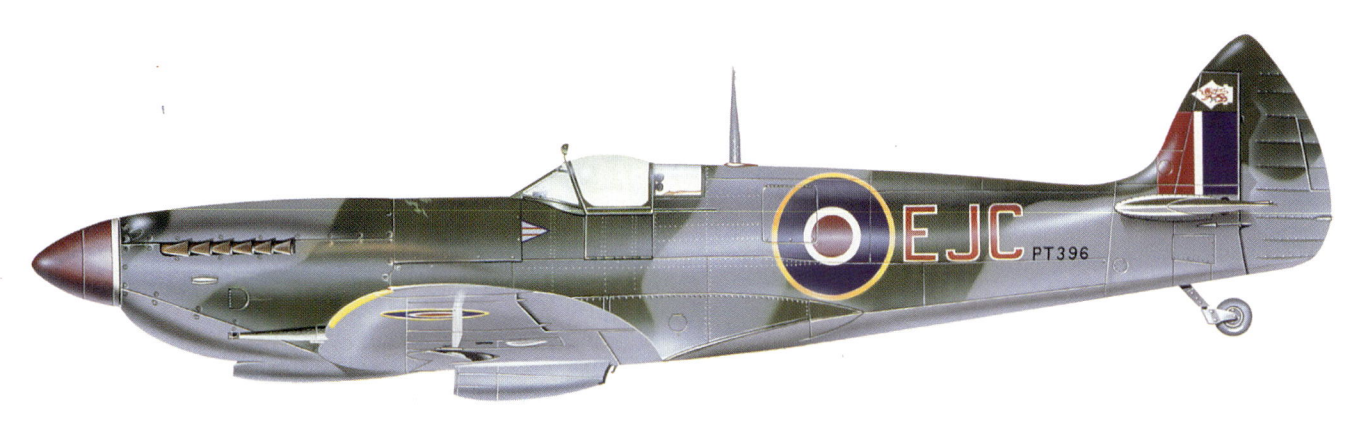

W/C E.F. "Jack" Charles, D.S.O., D.F.C. with bar, from Lashburn, Saskatchewan, flew this Spitfire IX (PT 396) in 1945. Charles claimed 15 victories during the war. The Tangmere crest is carried on the fin of this aircraft.

W/C James "Stocky" Edwards, D.F.C. with bar, of Saskatchewan, flew this Spitfire XVI (TD 147) during April 1945 in 127 Wing. Edwards scored 19 victories, making him one of the top Allied aces of the war.

W/C Stan Turner, D.S.O., D.F.C. with bar, flew this Spitfire XVI (TB 300) in 127 Wing during April 1945. Note that full rounded wingtips were installed, replacing the clipped wingtips.

W/C Jeff Northcott, D.S.O., D.F.C. with bar, from Minnedosa, Manitoba, flew this Spitfire XIV (MV 263) in 126 Wing during May 1945. Northcott scored nine victories during the war.

Don Morrison, D.F.M., D.F.C., flew this Spitfire IX (BS 119) in 401 Squadron during the Dieppe Raid on August 19, 1942. The aircraft carried his Jiggs cartoon insignia on the nose. When he was shot down, he was the leading RCAF ace with six aircraft destroyed and several probables and damaged. Morrison recalled that the aircraft had a nonstandard camouflage scheme—medium sea-grey and dark sea-grey, giving it an overall blue appearance.

Robert Morrow, D.F.C., from Alberta, flew this Spitfire V (BM 257) as leader of 402 Squadron during July 1942.

F/L Al Harley flew this Spitfire V (W3131), named DO II, in 401 Squadron during April 1942. This aircraft was one of several he named DO for his wife, Dorothy. Note the dark earth and grey camouflage on the upper surfaces, and the light grey on the lower surfaces.

George "Buzz" Beurling, D.S.O., D.F.C., D.F.M. with bar, from Verdun, Quebec, flew this Spitfire IX (MA 585) as his personal aircraft in 403 Squadron in September and October of 1943. He became Canada's top ace, and 29 of his victories are marked with small German crosses along the engine cowling.

From December 1943 to February 1944, in 412 Squadron, George "Buzz" Beurling also flew this Spitfire IX (MH 883) as his personal aircraft. Thirty of his victories are marked in swastikas along the nose of the aircraft.

F/O Jack Sheppard flew this Spitfire V (EN 921) as his personal aircraft in 401 Squadron during July 1943. Jack was later S/L of 412 Squadron. F/L "Ibby" Ibbotson flew the Spitfire V (W3834) (background) in July 1943.

F/L Len Thorne of Toronto flew this Spitfire IX (MJ 880) in 421 Squadron in June 1944. Thorne was one of the first pilots to land in France after D-Day.

Both F/L Larry Seath from Montreal and W/C R.A. Ellis, D.F.C., of 39 Reconnaissance Wing flew this Spitfire XI (PA 900) on D-Day. Later the D-Day stripes were partially removed, but left on the fuselage and bottom wing surfaces.

F/L "Sten" Lundberg was flying this Spitfire IX (MJ 832) in 416 Squadron on May 21, 1944, when he was forced down by flak.

Warren Middleton, D.F.C., from British Columbia, flew this Spitfire XIV, (FR) coded Z (RM 824), in 430 Squadron during April 1945. On April 17, 1945, he downed a FW 190 from this aircraft.

Norman Chevers from Niagara Falls flew this Spitfire IX, KH-J (MJ 986), during March 1944 in 403 Squadron.

S/L Bert Houle, D.F.C. with bar, C.D., from Massey, Ontario, flew this Spitfire VIII (JG 184) in 417 Squadron, based in Anzio, Italy, during February 1944.

F/L Guy Mott, D.F.C., from Sarnia, Ontario, flew this Spitfire IX (NH 209) in 441 Squadron in October 1944. Mott was one of the squadron's aces, scoring 5 1/2 victories.

F/L Hugh Ritchie from Toronto flew this Spitfire IX (MK 941) in 441 Squadron during September and October of 1944. Ritchie, who was an artist, designed the silver fox insignia for the 441 Squadron crest.

S/L Roy "Kelly" Walker from Niagara Falls flew this Spitfire IX (ML 345) in 441 Squadron during the Nijmegen campaign in September and October 1944.

F/L Jack Boyle, D.F.C., of Burlington, Ontario, flew this Spitfire IX in 411 Squadron from December 1944 to February 1945. The aircraft was named Sweet Sue V after his newborn daughter. He also carried a pair of her baby booties for good luck while on missions. Boyle was one of 411's aces, with 5 1/2 victories.

Denny Wilson from Toronto was flying this Spitfire IX, Israeli serial number 2015, in 101 Squadron, IDF, on December 31, 1948, when he shot down two Egyptian fighters. Wilson became an ace, with two RCAF victories and three victories with the IDF/AF during the war.

While returning from a fighter sweep on June 22, 1944, 442 Squadron was attacked by eight Me 109s. During the ensuing dogfight, P/O Bill Weeks from Loggieville, New Brunswick, flying a Spitfire coded Y2-D, scored the squadron's first victory.

F/L Brian "Blackie" MacConnell from Lindsay, Ontario, flew this Spitfire XIV (NH 703) in 402 Squadron in March 1945. The Spitfire, named Emily *after his wife, had previously been flown by Ernie Mouland.*

W/C Norm Bretz, D.F.C., flew this Spitfire V (EP 548), coded with his initials, from December 27, 1943, to March 26, 1944. Earlier, this Spitfire had been coded LV-C and flown by his friend Lloyd Chadburn. Note the late-style exhaust, rarely seen on Mark Vs.

F/L William Harper from Niagara Falls flew this Spitfire XVI (TB 886) in 421 Squadron during April 1945. Note that the aircraft carried the full code AU-J, but the A is not visible when the door is down. It was the first bubble-canopy Spitfire in 127 Wing and created a lot of interest.

F/L Ken Lawson of King City, Ontario, flew this Spitfire IX (MJ 351) in 414 Squadron in March 1945. This aircraft was later downed in action with pilot F/O W.A. Glaister, who managed to escape and make it back to base. The squadron badge shown here was not official until June 1960.

W/C "Johnnie" Johnson flew this Spitfire IX (MK 392) with Canadian 144 and 127 Wings during 1944 and early 1945. The aircraft is shown as it appeared in January 1945, with a TAF black spinner and a painted-over sky band.

F/L Ken Lawson from King City, Ontario, flew this Spitfire XIV (MV 348) in 414 Squadron in April 1945. The aircraft was named Violet-Dorothy III *after his mother and his wife.*

D-DAY, D-DAY, D-DAY

Cecil Brown, 403 Squadron

WHILE events on D-Day have been recorded by historians much more capable than I, I think I should quote the notes I wrote in my logbook when we finished flying that day.

"D-Day—June 6/44. Allies invade the Continent at points between Cherbourg Peninsula and Le Havre. Role of our Wing (127) is to provide close cover for the beachhead armies against enemy aircraft. First patrol from here over area at 0700 hrs for 50 minutes. All aircraft came back OK having seen no hun aircraft but apparently met some flak. G/C MacBrien flew with our Squadron. Day began rainy and cleared by 0830 hrs (Flying KH-N, serial NH 196).

"Next patrol over beach at 1200 hrs. Wing did four patrols today. Saw no Hun aircraft. All of ours OK. Naval and airborne forces a magnificent sight as they go towards beach. Hundreds of Dakotas towing gliders and carrying paratroops. Thunderbolts and Typhoons and Mustangs doing dive-bombing just inside beachhead. Hundreds of landing craft pouring into beach and an unbroken stream of naval craft all the way across the Channel. In addition to Spit Wings there are also T'Bolts, Mustangs and Lightnings covering beach and troops moving inland. Truly the 'Greatest Show on Earth,' and one well worth seeing. The organization for this must be terrific, but things seem to be going to plan."

I was flying KH-N (NH 196). When we left Tangmere and approached the Channel, I could hardly believe what I was seeing. Solid ships as far as one could see. I felt they were packed tight enough to make a landing strip. They were of all types: naval ships, merchant ships, landing craft, barges on tow—just about everything you could imagine. True to their reputation, the gunners on some of the ships fired at any aircraft they saw. Even though we were wearing the broad black and white stripes and were flying low enough for those to be seen, we drew a few ineffectual bursts while flying

Cecil Brown with Doug Orr's Spitfire IX, Eleanor. *Brown usually flew KH-N in 403 Squadron. June 1944.* – Cecil Brown

toward France. Even a couple of Lightnings made a pass at us, but they didn't fire.

As we approached the beach to take up our patrol stations I got that "you ain't seen nothing yet" feeling. German shells were bursting on the beach, and at the same time we could see our battleships firing 16-inch shells over the beach at targets beyond. All hell was erupting, and there we were at 1,500 feet flying up and down our sector, watching the show. Everyone seemed much too busy to bother with us, which was OK with us.

We could see a couple of American warships that had been hit and were beginning to list quite badly. They were right inshore and were sitting targets for shore batteries. The scene changed rapidly as we flew back and forth. We could see Allied soldiers moving up a lane

Spitfire DN-L in its D-Day stripes in Brazenville, France, on June 25, 1944. The sandy soil was picturesque, but the dust was very dangerous during operations. – DND PL 30299, Steve Sauvé

alongside a hedge and at the same time German troops coming at right angles to them along another hedge. There was no way we could warn our men, nor could we break our assigned task to dive down and give the Germans a squirt or two. An operation of this magnitude and complexity had to rely on strict discipline, and we could not just rush off even though the urge to help was overpowering.

The British had two huge "monitors"—really just massive gun platforms that had no engines and had to be towed into place. One was the *Roberts* and I believe the other was the *Rodney*. They were sitting out in the Channel, well offshore, and were pouring a steady stream of heavy shells on targets inland. Even at great distance the flashes from their guns were almost blinding. Everyone seemed to be shooting at everyone else, and we just flew along watching the whole thing.

We were at 1,500 feet and we learned that fighters were stacked above us up to 15,000 feet. The first few layers were only 100 feet apart, but higher up they were not so concentrated. No wonder there was little opposition from the Luftwaffe.

I observed all of this during the first patrol I was on, which was at about noon. On my second patrol, at 8 p.m., we could see that the American warships that had been listing at noon were now resting on the bottom, although the water was so shallow that they were mostly above water. This patrol was as uneventful as the others of the day, and I do not recall hearing of anyone in our wing firing his guns. The only danger was from the shells being lobbed in from the Channel—they had trajectories that made them pass perilously close to us. However, no one was hit by them.

On June 7, again our two teams flew two patrols each. The weather was quite hazy, and while we could not see far inland it appeared that the Allies were making progress. Few incidents spoiled our day, and we were not engaged by the enemy. I flew KH-V (MH 928) that day.

Johnny Drope of 421 Squadron was a great guy. He came from Winnipeg, and when we talked about what we would do after the war, he always said he was going to work for his uncle, who was the biggest bootlegger in Toronto. Johnny happened to be on the same shift as me, and while we were patrolling I heard him call his leader to say his engine was quitting. His C.O. advised him to bail out rather than try to land, as the beach was covered with trucks, tanks, jeeps, and all sorts of material.

With three squadrons flying as one wing, the chance of spotting a particular aircraft was pretty slim, but I just happened to be looking in Johnny's direction when I saw him jump over the side. I watched as he went down. His parachute never opened, and the splash his body made was as big as, if not bigger than, the one made by his aircraft. It was hard to keep from throwing up. We lost friends from time to time but I had never seen a person killed this way.

Later, Bob Grigg of 421 went missing, but as he didn't call out and no one saw him go, we never heard what happened. Our companion wing, the 126, got into a scrap with some Ju 88s that were trying to dive-bomb the beachhead and shot down six of them without loss. The Ju 88s were almost defenceless and it was pretty easy for the 126 guys to pick them off.

On June 8, the weather was quite poor. We were up at 3:15 a.m. to do standby. The same four shows were scheduled, but the last one had to be cancelled because of bad weather. I flew KH-R (MJ 886) that day.

Again I had the staggering experience of watching one of our guys die, and again it was over the beachhead. A fellow named Miranda in 416 Squadron had engine trouble and was advised by his C.O. to bail out. This time I think we all saw him going down. His chute was properly deployed and all he had to do, we thought, was wait a few minutes to be picked up. He landed in the water and the wind carried his chute well away from him. For some reason he was unable to release his chute and then we saw the undertow start to pull his chute under the surface. A rescue launch was racing toward him, but before it could reach him we saw his feet disappear below the surface.

For us the only bright spot of the day was that the Allied forces seemed to be making better progress, but of course that was just our observation from the air. I don't know what the official news was.

June 9 was completely overcast and all patrols were cancelled. However, there was so much complaining from the troops and the Navy about not having the patrols that it was decided about 7 p.m. to send one.

The weather was so bad that there was no way a whole wing of 36 aircraft could be dispatched. It would only create total confusion, so it was decided to send only one squadron of 12 aircraft. We in 403 got the honours.

We were hardly airborne when we were in clouds. At times the clouds were right down to the surface of the Channel, and as we headed for the beachhead we were in and out of them all the way, even though we were flying between 300 and 500 feet. From time to time we would break cloud, but most of the time it was impossible to know where the rest of the squadron was. It took the better part of half an hour to reach the beachhead, and as we approached the clouds began to show signs of breaking up. At last, the visibility improved slightly and we started to think that perhaps we could do a patrol, not at our usual height of 1,500 feet but somewhere between 500 and 1,000 feet. Just then a flak battery on one of the ships started to fire at us and right away the shit hit the fan.

After the first battery fired it took only a second before every bastard behind a flak gun joined in. The air was red with flak and we were the only targets. We could have all been shot down since we had thought we were in friendly territory and were not trying to evade.

The C.O. called a break, and we reassembled out of range of the guns that had opened fire. He called the controller, and after a couple of minutes we were assured that all was under control and asked if we would please give it another try. This time we got no farther than before when the flak began once more. Again we broke for safety.

We asked for help and were assured it was now safe, so back we went. This time the flak was thicker and more accurate, and Bill Williams was shot down and lost. Dean Kelly took a bullet splinter on the bottom edge of his armour plate right behind his back. Pieces of the bullet smashed into his buttocks and, although he was anything but comfortable, he was able to fly back to Tangmere.

When the firing began for the third time our C.O. just yelled, "Everybody break off and head home by yourself!" That we did, and except for Bill and Dean we all got back without further trouble. Dean's seat was full of blood when he landed, but after a few days he was able to fly again. When we assessed the damage we found that three others had been hit.

On June 10, our wing did four patrols over the beachhead as the weather had improved. All patrols were uneventful, and it seemed a bit incongruous for us to be watching the whole show below without getting involved. However, our job was still to defend the beach, and the fact that the Germans never attacked was proof that we were doing our job. I flew KH-N (NH 196) that day.

On June 11, on our first trip of the day, we landed in France for the first time. It was a bit of a shaky landing as the airstrip was still under construction and the bulldozers were still trying to smooth out a runway. The bulldozer operators had to be gutsy as they were working practically in view of the Germans. When the topsoil was peeled away it exposed a subsoil that had the consistency of flour, so that even the stamping of a foot caused a cloud to rise. Imagine the dust storm that was raised when a wing of Spitfires tried to land. I flew KH-P (MK 881) that day.

There was no turning back, so we went in, one after the other, hoping that no one was sitting on the ground ahead admiring his landing. The runway was very rough, and even after I set the aircraft down I was less than confident that all would turn out OK. Still, we all made it, and after refuelling and resting a while we did another patrol before going back to Tangmere. The only incident was that Andy MacKenzie was shot down by our own troops. But he landed alright and returned to us the next day.

Our chief medical officer, S/L Cam MacArthur, and our flying control officer, Reg Fisher, had different experiences. Reg got ashore but Cam's ship was torpedoed and he lost his driver and ambulance. As a result, he was given time to recover from his experience. He was replaced by Bill Metzler. Cam came around to Tangmere to say goodbye and that was the last we saw of him for some time. We had enjoyed a good relationship with Cam and it was sad to have him leave us just as the invasion was beginning. Bill Metzler was a good choice as his replacement, and we soon found a friend in him. At that time there was also a medical officer for each squadron. Our M.O. for 403 was Don Munro; 421 had Vic Perry and 416 had Jack McLean.

As the invasion neared, fellows who were near the end of their tours had been held over. Now, in view of the way things were going, those who were over the limit were beginning to be replaced. The first to leave was Jim Preston, on June 12.

The ground crew of 441 and 402 Squadrons were part of the 6441 Servicing Echelon at Douai in 1944. Left to right: Atkins, Bill Reale, Wise and Lacombe. – Bill Reale

Ground Crew

Bill Reale, Armourer, 441, 402 Squadrons
(armourer for "Johnnie" Johnson's aircraft)

THE armourers were considered the low-life of the whole ground crew, but if the guns hadn't been serviced properly, if they hadn't been in working order, the pilots would have had nothing to defend themselves with—they'd have had to high-tail it out. Once you missed a chance, you didn't get that chance again. We had very few gun stoppages. You might have had a malfunction or something, but I never heard of any.

Once, in Saint-Croix, one of the Spitfires was sitting at the edge of the field when all of a sudden, this gun started to go, just blasted away with no one in the cockpit. Something had gone wrong electrically—you should have seen this thing, just burping away!

A Spitfire's guns were all harmonized, because you wanted them to fire in a certain pattern. Before they were ready for combat, you had to set the aircraft in flying position. There was a sight for each of the guns on the aircraft, and you had to harmonize the guns according to where the pilot set his target. So, he'd set the bull's-eye on the outboard port gun, and you harmonized the barrel of that gun to that target.

The pilots all wanted a different cone of fire, because they all flew differently. Some of them wanted a smaller cone of fire, some of them wanted wider.

Adjustments were made according to the way each gun was mounted on the wing. You had your harmonizing rod, which was a small periscope that you stuck down the barrel. You sighted the target through that periscope, and while you were watching, your buddy was doing all the adjustments. Then you locked the gun in the desired position.

Each armourer did a little of everything. We were all trained to arm the bombs. There were 250-pounders and 500-pounders, and we were trained to put in the proper detonators according to a colour code, and the proper time delays. The bombs would have to be suspended on the aircraft so they'd drop either dead or live. If a pilot wanted to jettison his load and not blow anything up, he could drop it that way. When a pilot didn't carry his bomb under the wing, he often carried an underbelly gas tank, which was streamlined to offer less wind resistance.

There were usually two men for every three aircraft, except that W/C Johnson had a guy with him by the name of Jim Waters. When they formed 144 Wing, Waters was Johnson's armourer. I got to take his place when Waters had to go home on compassionate leave. I thought I must have been a damn good armourer for them to put me on Johnson's aircraft.

I was always conscientious. I don't know if you've seen my pictures, but they show me working on the wing, while all the other guys are hanging around shooting the bull.

Johnson had two aircraft. He had JEJ Junior, which he only took up a few times—he almost always relied on the other one, JEJ. JEJ Junior was there in case the other one wasn't ready. To make sure he got out there, we kept both of them going.

If you were in the "Flights," you were up where the aircraft took off and came back. Maintenance was where all the harmonizing and setting of the guns was done. There, the fellows on duty worked on every aircraft. It was the same with the other trades—the fitters, the engine mechanics, the radio people, whatever you had. Everything in maintenance was done the way the pilots wanted it done. In the flights, we just serviced them, like you would a car at a gas pump.

In June 1944, we landed in France on an American LST. We were the advance crew on the ground, and I was one of the advance crew armourers. They picked certain of us—just about half the armourers in each squadron, half the fitters, and half the riggers—so you had half the crew back at the airfield. The advance crew left by truck for the Salisbury Plain. We waterproofed our vehicles in case we had to go down into the water from the LST.

We got on board at Gosport, which I think is part of Plymouth harbour—drove our trucks down the concrete causeway and into the hold of that LST. Then we just sailed out into the Channel and waited our turn to get out. Sitting there, we could see all the action overhead, and all the action inland, too. You could hear the cannons, you could hear the *Rodney* letting go her 15-inch guns. It scared the hell out of me on one—I couldn't believe what I heard! You could see dogfights, you could see guys bailing out of Flying Fortresses, Spitfires being shot down. You could see all the flak up in the air from the anti-aircraft guns.

The LST landed with the high tide, and when the water went out, it was all dry to land. At one point the driver we were with took a wrong turn because there was so much dust. We ended up in a place with no one in front of us! We turned around and went back. I think we had been to an area that we shouldn't have.

We slept in the grain fields because they were not mined at the time. There were, however, a lot of bomb craters in there, and all the fields were laid with this wire mesh for the Spitfires. The army engineers had done that. We landed on the beach six days after D-Day, June 12, which was three days before Johnson and his gang landed there. So the ground crew was there three days before the pilots. The ground crew's rear group came over on DC-3s, also on June 15.

I don't think anyone's put it down on paper —I have never seen it written in any of the stories—but it went around like wildfire in Normandy that Wally McLeod had shot down two Jerries, and he only used 17 rounds of cannon shell out of each gun to do it.

Johnson got up the next day as soon as he could. A while later he came roaring back, swung that Spitfire around, and with the cockpit coupe top opened up he was yelling at me, "How many rounds did I use?" I jumped up on the wing (I had my boots on instead of my sneakers, which I was supposed to have), lifted open the ammo tank, and I said, "You damn near used them all!"

He had shot down his two aircraft, but he was upset that he had used so much ammo, and that I had the wrong shoes on. However, all was forgiven.

It always seemed to me that we in 144 Wing were like guinea pigs. While we had leaders like Johnnie Johnson, and our pilots were very capable, our wing, in general, had the least amount of experience. Other wings had been training for years in England, but our fellows had only recently been flying in Canada. Yet it was the first to land in Normandy. I suspect that they expected heavy losses, and that we were the most expendable if casualties were high. As soon as the D-Day invasion was a success, they broke up 144 Wing, yet it had the best record in that invasion of all the wings.

When 441 Squadron was sent home, we in the ground crew stayed on and looked after the 402 and their Mark XIVs. So there was no rest period or relief for the hard-working guys in the ground crew.

"JOHNNIE" JOHNSON'S THIRTY-THIRD VICTORY

Guy Mott, 441 Squadron

On June 30, 1944, we went up about noon, from B3 strip in France. Johnnie Johnson, in 9G-W (NH 320—Tommy Brannagan's aircraft), was leading the flight that I was in. The other flight was led by our squadron leader, Danny Browne (9G-C, ML 205), who was on his last flight with the 441 before his tour expired. There were twelve aircraft altogether, split into two flights of six.

We were on an armed recce near Falaise, and I was flying my aircraft, 9G-K (PL 274), on the port side of Johnnie. My No. 2 was Jack Copeland (MK 992). We were above clouds and on the lookout for some enemy aircraft that had been reported.

Suddenly, through the clouds, we saw these enemy aircraft passing just beneath us. Copeland and I went down after them, after reporting them. Johnson couldn't yet see them from where he was, but since we had, he gave the OK for us to go after them.

The ones that we had seen—well, they were just the front of the enemy group. We fell in behind them, but the rest of the enemy (they were Me 109s) were then behind us. It became a great turnaround.

Johnson knew we were down there, but since he was above cloud, he couldn't see us. Finally he and his No. 2, Bob Draper (MK 504), were able to come down with the rest of the flight, and we all ended up in this big melee, going around and around. I got one destroyed, but my No. 2 had his aircraft damaged by enemy fire. Other fellows got scores. F/L A. Johnstone (9G-B, ML 269) destroyed one and damaged one. Browne also had a destroyed.

During the battle, Johnson got his thirty-third, while Draper covered him. Finally, the melee was over, and we turned back to base. My No. 2, Copeland, made a successful landing with one wheel down. Chowan (9G-A, MJ 344) was badly shot up. We were sad to lose P/O Fleming (9G-Q, MK 737). We didn't know what happened to him. He may have become a P.O.W.

In 144 Wing, Johnson didn't fly with us all the time—he took turns going from one squadron to the other, but on this day, he was flying with us. It was a significant air battle because in it Johnson surpassed Sailor Malan's record of kills and became the number-one ace.

Guy Mott, with his aircraft, 9G-K (NH 209), in October 1944. – Guy Mott

"Johnnie" Johnson

Bill Weeks, 442 Squadron

All who flew with Johnnie Johnson will remember him as an exceptional pilot and an outstanding fighter leader. Many of us will also recall with pleasure his subtle sense of humour.

We pilots of 144 Wing had known for several days that we would be moving to B3, at Saint-Croix-sur-Mer in Normandy, sometime during the morning of June 15. B3 was located in a large pasture; sod had been removed and wire mesh laid down to form a runway. It was a suitable enough landing strip, albeit exceedingly dusty.

In view of this, Johnson decided that we would make our move one squadron at a time, at about 30-minute intervals. He selected S/L B.D. Russel's 442 Squadron to go first.

We landed in pairs, with enough intervals between pairs to allow the dust to clear, and dispersed our aircraft. Shortly thereafter, a lone Spitfire flew over the field. It was low enough that we could read the letters JEJ on its side—Johnson's letters. On his first approach, Johnson did not come close to getting his aircraft down, nor did he on the second. He did grease it on during his third or fourth attempt—in my mind it was the latter—and parked near our aircraft.

He walked over to where Russel was standing and was overheard to say, "Dal, if I hadn't gotten the darn thing down on that last approach, I was going to get you to send up one of your boys to shoot me down."

On June 30, 1944, W/C "Johnnie" Johnson was flying S/L Tommy Brannagan's Spitfire IX, 9G-W (NH 320), from 441 Squadron when he scored his 33rd victory. F/O Bohemier is in the foreground.
– Hugh Ritchie

"A Short While Into the Sun"

Bill Weeks, 442 Squadron

On the morning of June 15, 1944, 144 Wing moved to France and began operating from B3 at Saint-Croix-sur-Mer. On the evening of June 18, a vicious Atlantic storm, which would last for three and a half days, struck the Normandy beaches, causing great destruction to our off-loading facilities. At noon of June 22, the day was bright and the sun high. Johnnie Johnson briefed 442 Squadron and one of the other squadrons of the wing and placed us on readiness. During the briefing, I was assigned to fly No. 2 to F/L Deane Dover. Soon after, we were scrambled. We got airborne in good time, climbed to 12,000 feet, and flew in a southerly heading in the general direction of Argentan.

We had been on our heading for a very few minutes when Dover called Johnson on the R.T. and informed him that he had spotted aircraft below at a distance of six to eight miles. Johnson detached our section to check these aircraft out. Dover took us down in a gentle dive roughly on the same southerly heading for possibly two or three minutes, during which time we picked up air speed. He then began a medium 180-degree turn to the left. When we came out of that turn, we were about 300 yards behind a flight of four Me 109s.

Dover then attacked the leader of that flight. I skidded my aircraft about 75 yards to the left of him in order to give him good coverage. While getting into position, I glanced over my right shoulder and saw, closing rapidly, another flight of four 109s.

The leader of this second flight immediately began to attack Dover. Now the correct procedure for me would have been to alert Deane by calling for a break. Unfortunately, someone was nattering on the R.T., and all I could do was fire a burst from an angle of about 45 degrees at this aircraft that was attacking Dover, in order to divert the pilot.

I must have diverted him, for almost immediately, I noticed that I was overtaking that aircraft very rapidly, and was in danger of

Bill Weeks, 442 Squadron, in his Spitfire IX, Y2-D (MK 416), summer 1944. – DND PL 28947

overshooting it and getting myself shot down. I immediately closed my throttle and applied alternately left and right rudder, and did succeed in slowing down enough to end up in close formation with that Jerry aircraft.

My starboard wing overlapped his port wing, so from his cockpit to mine could not have been more than 20 feet. He seemed to be a tall, angular type, and he was obviously not perturbed by my presence, for he jabbed his left index finger at me with the thumb pointing downward, indicating to me (I suppose) where he thought I was going to go. I had the temerity to shake my head. Since we were in close formation, with our throttles closed, and rapidly losing air speed, it must have occurred to him that his 109 would stall before my Spitfire, for he suddenly opened his throttle. Before I could react

This 442 Squadron Spitfire IX, Y2-K (MK 304), was fitted with a new engine on August 19, 1944, during service in the field. – DND PL 31361

and get my throttle open, he was about 60 yards in front of me.

At about 75 yards, I lined him up carefully and opened fire. I could see the cannon shells striking the cockpit area and glycol vapour coming from the engine. The pilot must have been hit, for the aircraft went into a steep dive. I watched it briefly, and it then occurred to me that those other seven Messerschmitts were probably on my tail!

I proceeded to do a steep turn to the left. My turn was so tight that I missed a head-on collision with one of the 109s attacking me by a few yards; as a matter of fact, I was close enough to see smoke coming from the cannon in the nose cone of that aircraft. Meanwhile, I heard Dover inform the wing commander that his No. 2 had just been shot down and that he was rejoining the formation. I called Dover and told him that it was a Jerry I had shot down, and that I was all right except that I was rather busy at the moment. While being chased around in this big steep turn, I got in the odd wild shot and expended most (if not all) of my ammunition.

I was, to put it euphemistically, quite willing to terminate the engagement, except I had no idea how! The reflection of the sun in my rearview mirror suddenly brought to my mind a book I had read called *Signed With Their Honour*. The words on the flyleaf quickly came to mind: "And they journeyed a short while into the sun, and left the vivid sky signed with their honour." Immediately, I knew how to break off the action—I would continue my turn until I was facing into the sun, which was still high at that time of the afternoon, and point the nose of the Spitfire into the sun, and climb away.

This I did. My angle of climb was steeper than that of the Me 109s, and I could see in my rearview mirror that they were having difficulty in lining me up. When I reached about 8,000 feet, I looked off my starboard wing and saw Spitfires diving out of the blue.

Dover, as usual, had done the correct thing: realizing that a lone aircraft could have little effect, he had brought the rest of the formation back with him, and they proceeded to shoot down another five aircraft. "There were eight of them," said Johnson, "and we got six!"

Close Combat

I.F. "Hap" Kennedy, D.F.C., 401 Squadron

On July 2, 1944, 401 Squadron was on a mission led by S/L Lorne Cameron. It was a dive-bombing show. Red Section had just dropped its bombs when a Jerry bounced Blue Section. Blue just dropped its bombs, but the Jerry got away. So we ended up looking for other targets. I was flying a Spitfire IX that day (NH 247).

Flying north toward Caen, I saw about 30 Me 109s above our squadron. We immediately attacked, climbing up into them, and I got behind a section of five of them. From 150 yards, with only my machine guns working, my cannons having jammed, I fired good strikes on a 109, until I was out of ammunition.

The 109's engine was dead, and the pilot was perhaps injured. I flew alongside him, very close, and he looked at me. He had on a tropical helmet (light fabric), so he may have been in the Middle East, as I had been earlier. I signalled him to turn around and glide north, as I wanted to get him down on our side of the lines. He did a gliding U-turn of 180 degrees, but we were losing height rapidly, and he waved frantically that he was going to crash, and he made a belly landing, damaging his aircraft considerably in the process. I took some gun camera pictures of the 109 and always hoped he might have survived the crash. [This was Kennedy's twelfth victory, and won him a bar for his D.F.C.]

I was made S/L of 401 Squadron on July 3, 1944, the day after Cameron was shot down by ground fire while strafing a convoy of vehicles near Falaise. But I did not last long either; three weeks later, on July 26 while flying (MK 311), I was shot down by flak during an attack on Dreux aerodrome. I had to bail out.

Evading capture in France that August was an exhilarating experience. I was helped by the Maquis (underground) with a false passport, and had some close calls with German troops, but I was lucky and was back in England in a month.

George Keefer's Spitfire IX, GC-K (MK 826), the lead of 126 Wing, 1944. Note how the stripes on the underwing stop short of the leading edge of the wing. – DND RE68-1159, Steve Sauvé

My successor in 401 Squadron, S/L H.C. Trainor, D.F.C., had just been forced down (near Eindhoven on 19 September) and was a P.O.W. It seemed likely I would resume my command of the squadron, but it was not to be. My younger brother had just been killed, so Air Marshall Breadner decided to send me back to Canada.

After the rain at de Rips, the Netherlands. Cecil Mann of the ground crew took this photograph of YO-W (MJ 448), flown by S/L Rod Smith in October 1944. – Cecil Mann

Stu Tosh's Spitfire IX, KH-T (MK 857), was hit by flak on July 19, 1944. The 403 Squadron aircraft carried D-Day stripes underwing and on the fuselage bottom. In the foreground, an American GI is looking for mines with a detector—a hazardous occupation. – DND PL 31127

Down in a Minefield

Stu Tosh, 403 Squadron

I wouldn't want to try it again. On July 19, 1944, I was on a front-line patrol with Cec Brown, Reg Thompson, Larry Wilcocks, Ken Harvey, and Ken Oliver. North of Saint-Lô, we were fired at by American A.A. We continued on north to Isigny, where we were fired at again by the Americans. When I got hit, I was smoking real badly, and all I thought about was putting the thing down in a field that looked suitable.

The wings of a Spitfire slope up a little bit to the outside tips, and since I was smoking so badly, I could not see very well. I came down fast and skidded through the first field, then hit a ditch. I turned 90 degrees but still kept sliding in the same direction. Finally, I stopped and I jumped out of the plane. I didn't even take the parachute off—I just jumped out of the plane.

It was a Black American A.A. battery that shot me down. They hit five out of six of us and shot three of us down! Cec Brown landed safely at A3, and Reg Thomson came down at A10, wounded. We had only been at 600 feet, so they had a good shot at us. I was between Saint-Lô and the English Channel at Isigny when I was hit.

I knew enough to run back along the skid marks that my Spitfire, KH-T (MK 857, my usual plane), had made. At the same time, the Black troops that were on the other side of the canal were shouting at me, "Don't move! Don't move!" And then I realized it was a minefield! I was on the west side of a canal, and the Americans came across in little rafts, searching the area with mine detectors. You can see one of them in the photo on the opposite page.

I had passed over two of these mines—they had passed just underneath my wing—and a third was wedged right under my wing, as you can see in one of the photos I have. So on top of being shot down, I had nearly been blown up three times!

Anyway, I got out OK. When I got across the canal I found a ride from there to Bayeaux in a half-track. That's as far as it could go, so I got out and proceeded to walk down the main street of Bayeaux with a parachute over my shoulder and my helmet and everything. A jeep stopped. There was a wing commander in it, and he said, "What's going on?" It looked kind of strange for a pilot to be walking down a street with a parachute. I don't remember his name, but he drove me back to B2 airfield at Crépon.

When I arrived back there, it was close to seven o'clock. I had been missing for four hours. "Iron Bill" McBrien was the C.O. of the station, and Johnnie Johnson, the RAF ace, was there. Doug Lindsay from Arnprior was one of the flight commanders, and the other flight commander was Andy MacKenzie.

Nowadays they would call it "friendly fire." However, I was not as unlucky as MacKenzie, who was shot down twice by the Americans—once in the Second World War, and once in Korea, where he was a P.O.W. However, at the time I was just glad to get back to our billets, which were in an apple orchard. I was soon back on operations.

Jamie Jamieson, left, and Wilf J. Banks, centre, just after they shot down a German Me 109. Jack Sheppard is on the right. Wilf recalled, "We were looking at a piece of flak." – Hugh Ritchie

On June 11, 1944, F/O H.G. Garwood of 412 Squadron suffered an engine failure. He managed to return to his squadron a few days later. His Spitfire IX, VZ-S (MJ 255), is shown here on June 17, 1944. Passing by are Canadian Shermans moving up for the attack on Tilly-sur-Seulles. – IWM B5660

THREE IN ONE MISSION

Wilfred Banks, D.F.C., 412 Squadron

IT had rained for three days, so there wasn't much activity until July 24, 1944.

As near as I can remember, this is what happened that day. Four of us took off that afternoon to check the weather conditions over the battle area. We were also carrying 250-pound bombs under each wing to bomb a bridge in the Lisieux area. I was flying Black No. 4. F/L O.M. Linton was leading (MJ 147). P/O D.R. Jamieson (NH 346) and F/L H.L. Phillips (VZ-V, MK 237) were also along. My aircraft was VZ-N (MJ 485), as usual.

I don't remember what happened to the bombs. About 35 miles into enemy territory, ground control warned us of enemy planes in the area. Moments later, we saw a group of Hun planes crossing our path about three miles ahead. We altered course about 20 degrees and opened our throttles to close in on them.

My comrades saw the situation as 20-plus enemy fighters—109s and 190s—who were soon joined by a further 20 or so fighters. The way I saw it, there were about 20 in the main group, but about 3,000 feet above, there were perhaps about six more, who were giving top cover to the main group. This was a common tactic employed by the Luftwaffe; they hoped we would become engrossed with the main group, so that the cover group could get in behind us.

It was soon apparent that these Germans intended to do battle with us; I could see the engine smoke as they opened their throttles. They started a wide port turn to form a continuous wheel-like formation so that they were protecting each other's tails. At this point, it became every man for himself, which seemed to me to be a better option than flying willy-nilly into the main group.

A Hun saw me coming and broke around to port to engage me. He was too late in his turn and I was able to get inside him and open up with my 20 mm cannons and 303 machine guns. About a quarter-second burst scored immediate hits, and he exploded in flames (as witnessed by Phillips).

[While this was happening, F/L Linton, leading the force, blew up one FW 190, which crashed near a road. He then blew half the port wing off another. P/O Jamieson destroyed two 109s: the first broke in two just behind the cockpit; the second exploded when it crashed near the cathedral in Lisieux.]

I now dived toward the main group, which was beginning to scatter. I started an attack but was attacked myself by a 109 coming from above. I broke around in a tight, climbing turn and overtook him. Once again, I fired about a quarter-second burst, and he exploded in flames.

By this time, the sky was a mass of aircraft wheeling in all directions. The formation was breaking up, and my situation was critical because it was difficult to see in all directions at once. In fact, a 109 was attacking me from below at about nine o'clock—I could see his guns flashing and trailing smoke, and his tracer bullets curling away behind me like a water hose. He could not sustain his climbing turn and promptly dived away.

It was about now that I saw a 109 spinning down with its entire tail section missing. I speculated that one of his buddies had got too close to him and chopped off his tail. Suddenly, the planes were all gone, and I was alone in an empty sky except for a lone 190, about 2,000 feet below and heading for Germany. With my height advantage and speed, and with surprise on my side, he had no chance. I closed to about 300 yards and fired a short burst, and he also exploded in flames.

My logbook says the battle lasted about 15 minutes, but it is hard to tell because you lose track of time under those conditions. It seemed to me that I had been going at full throttle for about 30 minutes. Anyway, I headed for home base and landed without further excitement.

[Note: Despite odds of ten to one, they had destroyed seven of the enemy.]

A Spitfire IX, VZ-M (PV 202), in its original 412 Squadron markings. This aircraft was restored in Dunsfold, England, February 23, 1990. – Peter Arnold

A German V-1 pilotless bomb at a 1945 victory display in London. – W.J. Bracken

A Spitfire XIV, AE-M (RM 689). This aircraft was later famous at airshows with Rolls-Royce sponsorship. In 402 Squadron, RM 689 was also coded D. The man in the photo, named Wyman, was the armourer who serviced AE-M in October 1944. – Bill Reale

Shooting Down a V-1 Flying Bomb

Bill Austin, 402 Squadron

IN 1944, the Germans began launching the V-1 pilotless bombs, or "Doodlebugs," against England. Shortly after, to counter this new menace, our squadron, 402, was moved to Hawkinge, Kent. We received the brand-new Spitfire XIV in August of that year. We had been at Merston, flying Mark IXs.

The Spitfire XIV gave us a real speed advantage—you were looking at 440 miles an hour at cruising altitude—and I'm sure that's why we got them. They were the hottest propeller-driven airplane at that time. With them, our squadron managed to shoot down a few V-1s.

We didn't see that many of them—they weren't coming over in droves, although the Germans launched quite a few of them. We patrolled over the Channel, and when we did see them, we could see them fairly well.

On August 23, 1944, I was flying out of Hawkinge in AE-G (RM 687) when our squadron encountered two or three of them. There was no problem catching up to them. The height at which they usually came in was around 3,000 feet. We'd usually be at 4,000 or 5,000 feet so we had the speed of the Mark XIV, plus a couple of thousand feet of diving. This way it was not too hard to get onto them.

My V-1 was about eight miles from Ashfield when I gave it a five-second burst. Fortunately, I suppose, it didn't blow up—there were just some pieces that flew off, and it turned down and ended up on the ground.

There was always the worry that attacking one would cause it to explode, taking you with it. I don't know of anyone being so unfortunate. There may have been some who ran into the debris, but that wasn't much different from shooting down any other enemy aircraft. If you were very close, and you got into the gas tank—of an Me 109, for example—you had the same problem: you had to evade very quickly if you could.

There was a Polish squadron across the field from us at Hawkinge—I think they had almost a point of honour that they wouldn't shoot these things down. Instead, they would slip a wing under the V-1's wing, and tip it. That threw off the gyro, causing the bomb to crash. What happened was that you ended up with an airframe that wasn't as good as it should be, particularly at the wing. Our Spitfire XIVs were valuable machines, and replacements were slow coming, so we were told not to do it that way. The Polish guys—they were madmen.

Bill Harvey and I had two of the interceptions of flying bombs, but we never did get any more. We saw two off Cap Grenier, but the one I knocked down was the only one I had a go at that I knew was destroyed.

After we did our stint at Hawkinge on the V-1s we ended up in Holland. I think George Lawson (AE-D, RM 689) and I (RM 734) were the first in our squadron to run into the Me 262 jets, on October 12, 1944. We were vectored onto this darn thing, and we were up sun, with everything in our favour. We started down the way it went, but we never did fire—it was so fast, neither of us was able to get a shot. The Germans were probably picking up our R.T., or maybe they were warned. At any rate, it was the only jet I ever saw in the air when I was in the service. Thank goodness there were not very many.

Most of the guys had their own airplanes after a while. Mine was coded AE-J. The C.O., of course, had his own aircraft. If yours was unserviceable, or needed for a 30-hour check, or something like that, then you went up in something else, but for the most part, you ended up in the same one.

R & R THE HARD WAY

Les Foster, 443 Squadron

THE action started to pick up again, and on July 3, 1944, we were scrambled to intercept a radar plot, and engaged more than 40 Me 109s down on the deck southeast of Alençon. I was flying No. 2 (MJ 741) on our C.O., Wally McLeod, D.S.O., D.F.C., and bar. McLeod had 20 Jerries destroyed to his credit. He was flying 2I-E (MK 636) that day.

C.O. Wally McLeod, 443 Squadron, with his Spitfire IX, 21-E (MK 636), June 1944.

– George Greenough

A pair of 109s broke out of the swarm and streaked to the south, with the S/L and me in hot pursuit. McLeod was always tenacious, and it was two minutes or so before he caught up with the nearest one and smartly put a few bullets into it. The Jerry promptly pulled up and bailed out—his plane crashed below him. The Jerry element leader broke left, and I quickly broke left, to stay inside his turn, at the same time calling for the C.O. to do the same.

No sooner did I break than a 20 mm explosive from an excellent (or lucky) Jerry A.A. battery came through the datum point on the left side of my cockpit, hit the armour plating in back of me, and exploded. The cockpit was immediately filled with smoke and the sound of the explosion temporarily deafened me, so I could not see or hear anything. A piece of the nose of the 20 mm had gone across behind me and had taken out my R.T. connection, so I could not talk to anybody. As this was not one of my favourite positions to be in, I promptly pulled up and jettisoned my coupe top, preparing to bail out.

As soon as the air rushed by the open cockpit and suctioned out the smoke, I realized that I had not gone blind. The effects of the explosion quickly wore off, and I could hear my Rolls-Royce Merlin purring away, so I realized that I did not need to pack up. It didn't take me too long to figure that it would be easier to fly back to my base than to walk back from far behind Jerry lines. So I set course for Crépon and put the kite down on the metal tracking at B2. Home again.

The flight surgeon took six chunks of shrapnel out of my left buttock, left a couple of pieces in me as a reminder, and kept me in the hospital for nine days. The best parts of the whole sortie were that I got ten days of R & R in Torquay, and McLeod got his Hun. It was his twenty-first confirmed kill, making him the RCAF's highest-scoring fighter pilot.

Les Foster with his usual Spitfire 2I-X (MJ 799), 443 Squadron, September 1944. – Les Foster

Ed Ferguson's last operational Spitfire, a Mark XVI, (SM 383). Previously he had flown a Spitfire IX, (ML 184). Ferguson always flew "P" as his aircraft in 443 Squadron. – Ed Ferguson

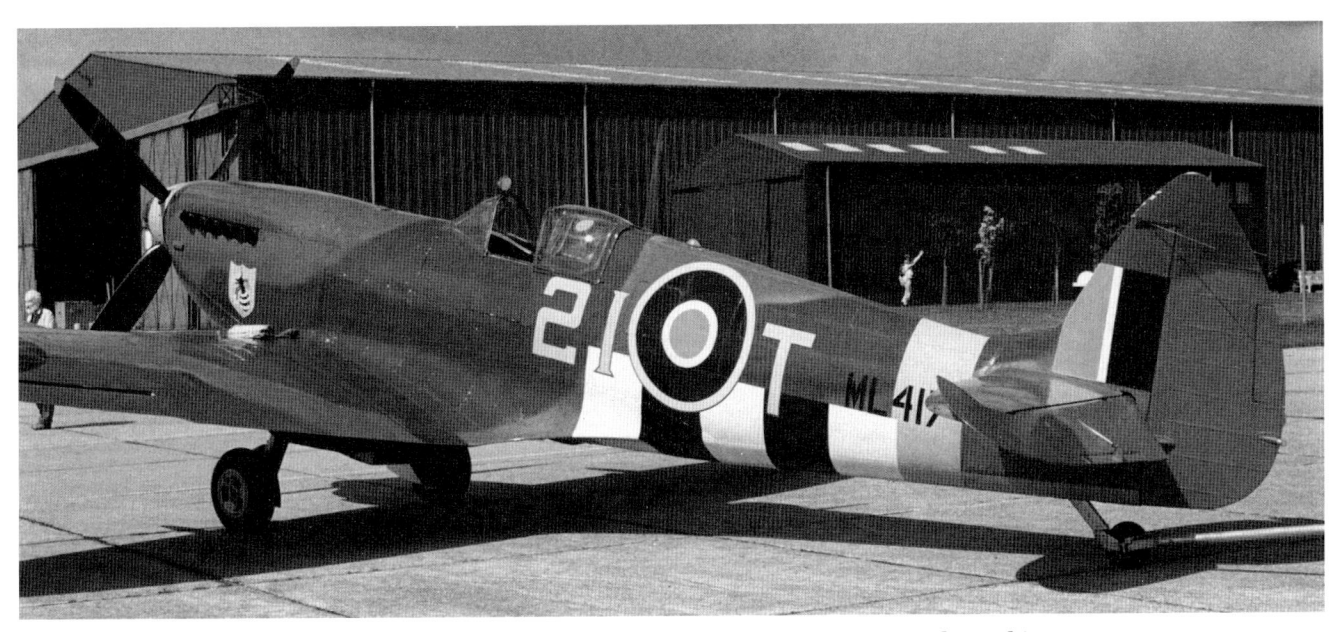

Spitfire IX, 2I-T (ML 417), of 443 Squadron, with its authentically restored markings. Duxford, England, I.W.M. Collection, June 1994. – R. Bracken

NIJMEGEN

"Kelly" Walker, 441 Squadron

AFTER leaving 416 Squadron when I became tour-expired, I assumed some non-flying duties, and then was given a month's leave back in Canada. I was told to expect to report to an operational fighter unit upon completion of my all-too-brief respite from the fighting. It was not a matter of volunteering. When I did go back, I asked for some Spitfire flying time before joining an operational unit. This was an unexpected move on my part, apparently. I am grateful that Johnnie Johnson told the brass to give me what I wanted. A new Spitfire was placed at my disposal.

The reason I dug my heels in about some practice time on the Spitfire is that it took some time to get prepared for combat. I had not flown a Spit in nine months, and I had heard of another experienced pilot who went right back into combat after an absence, and was quickly shot down when he blacked out in a combat with some Me 109s. He was too good a pilot to be shot down so easily. In combat, it is normal to lose consciousness in tight turns, but the body seems to be able to handle these stresses if given time to toughen up to the rigours and demands of combat flying. After practising with the Spit, I felt in better shape. I also went over gyro-sighting, air-to-ground flying and firing, and dive-bombing. After a week of this, I was ready for action.

I did not have long to wait. After a short stint with 403 Squadron, I took over command of the 441 when its C.O., Tommy Brannagan, went missing. We were based at forward airstrips in France, supporting the invasion forces. The advance was incredibly rapid, and we moved forward from Tilley to Beauvais, to Brussels, to Antwerp in a matter of days. The airfields just had numbers, like B19, B40, and B52, but each number was bringing us closer to the Rhine.

On September 17, 1944, I made my first flight into Germany, in my Spit IXb, 9G-W (ML 345). The next day, flying 9G-K (ML 370), we were protecting the Nijmegen bridge across the Rhine. The 109s of the Luftwaffe made an appearance, and I shared one destroyed with F/L George Johnstone. F/O Heisman destroyed another.

On another mission the same day, I was flying 9G-Y (NH 176), and again we encountered enemy aircraft. F/L Ron Lake destroyed a 109, flying 9G-L (ML 317), his usual aircraft.

Over the next few days I was constantly in action on missions to the Nijmegen bridge. My logbook shows I was flying 9G-W (ML 345), my usual aircraft. On September 25 special orders came to protect the bridge at all costs. There was increasing worry that the Germans would try to destroy it. Well, on that day, our nine aircraft ran into 30-plus Huns. Some were carrying bombs. Our squadron claimed three 109s destroyed and five damaged. I personally claimed two damaged. Most important is that we forced the enemy to drop their bombs short of the bridge, possibly saving the structure for the Allied advance. It was at a cost: this fight against superior odds cost us F/Sgt. McMillan (NH 151) and F/L Boe (ML 360). First they were reported missing, later we learned they had been killed.

My day was not over, for that evening I was back in 9G-W (ML 345), escorting C-47s dropping supplies to airborne troops at Arnhem bridge. We were timed to arrive at dusk, but even so, the seven transports faced terrible flak from the German defences, since they had to fly in at only about 500 feet. The flak was accurate and intense. We could see some of the ground combat from our Spitfires, but it was soon dark, and we returned to our base (B70) at Antwerp that night.

The next morning I was back over the Nijmegen Bridge. This time I encountered an Me 262 jet. I had a go, but it had an enormous speed advantage over me and left me like I was standing still. We continued to fly patrols in the area until September 30, 1944, when we were recalled back to Hawkinge, England.

The war was not over, for we continued to escort bombers as far as the Dutch–German border. At that time I had my "own" Spitfire, an older Mark Vb we had "found" in France. I had my own initials painted on it—RHW—instead of code letters. It was stripped of guns, armour and other equipment. What a difference it made. It was a very sweet ship, very light on the controls and responsive. It served as a squadron hack until one of the pilots damaged a wing. The RAF station commander made quite a fuss and asked all kinds of embarrassing questions. I could have been in a lot of trouble, as they were threatening court-martial and all kinds of things. Fortunately, this controversy soon blew over.

There were hazards other than combat. I took it upon myself to test aircraft after repairs. I did not wish to delegate this responsibility to younger, less experienced pilots. About this time, I took up a Spitfire that had just received a new aileron. I went through the preflight quickly, as everything seemed to be working. Unfortunately, I was not thorough enough, as the aircraft on takeoff wanted to turn left, when I turned right! Very quickly, I realized that the controls were rigged in reverse! The mechanics had made a mistake. A less experienced pilot might have been killed on takeoff. After that, for a long while, my preflight check was very thorough indeed.

On October 9, 1944, I flew my first Spitfire XIV, which was a really hot new weapon, and very powerful with the new Griffon engine. However, we continued to fly the Mark IXb, and flew the newer Mark XVI, which was basically the same plane but with a Packard-built Merlin. The Mark XVI was less popular, as it had some reported engine failures.

The 441 Squadron continued to escort bombers, mainly Lancasters, to targets in the Ruhr. On April 11, we escorted 125 Lancasters to Bayreuth, just north of Nurnberg, a long way into Germany. My logbook shows I flew 9G-E (MA 528). This time, there was no flak and we

The 441 Squadron transport car, which travelled all over Europe and eventually found its way back home to Canada. – R.H. Walker

saw no fighters. I wrote in my logbook, "I think the Hun has had it." On April 18, we escorted 1,000 Lancs to bomb an island of about one square mile in Heligoland. What a pasting!

On April 29, the squadron moved again, this time to Hunsdon, England. Shortly after, we began to receive Mustang III aircraft. Our squadron was to reequip with the Mustang. I continued flying the Mustang until July 27, 1945, when my war ended. I had a total flying time of 843 hours, with total ops time of 330 hours and 220 sorties.

As a Second World War Spitfire pilot, I found that to survive I had to be able to think quickly and clearly under pressure with little time to make decisions. A really good pilot had to develop something more—a "sixth sense" that kept him alive. I certainly feel that my many months of combat heightened that sense.

How I Shot Down a 109

Sid Bregman, 441 Squadron

On September 27, 1944, we were patrolling the area around Arnhem, at about two in the afternoon, as a squadron. We all had special long-range tanks on the underside of our aircraft, which gave us some additional range, because we were stationed at Antwerp at the time. Normal range was 80 to 90 minutes at the most. Those tanks gave us an extra hour.

In any case, while we were patrolling over Arnhem, my engine stopped. Obviously the tank had fallen off, so I switched immediately. That particular manoeuvre put me in a position somewhat astern of the rest of the squadron, although my wingman was still with me. As I looked over my shoulder, lo and behold, there was an Me 109 alone, with me now very manoeuvrable because I didn't have that tank. It took about two or three seconds for me to get in line, and another second or two after that I hit the 109. That was the end of it—it only took 11 shells altogether. Just a quick burst and it went down immediately. Because I'd lost the tank, I got permission from the squadron leader to head back to Antwerp. My kill was confirmed later by Don Kimball. Apparently, the 109 crashed into the Rhine at Arnhem. We had done a lot of air-to-ground, but that was my first German aircraft.

My wingman and I went back very quickly, flying fairly low because we were concerned about being exposed. My wingman came along to give me some protection because we were alone over enemy territory. There was a lot of activity going on in the Arnhem area. I remember flying over a bombed-out city—I could tell it was Cologne by the cathedral with the twin spires. Our navigation was very primitive; we just had the general direction and some landmarks to follow. In any case, we landed safely at Antwerp.

We were heavily involved in the Falaise Gap. The Battle of the Bulge was going on and we were supporting the ground troops quite heavily. One day, at seven in the morning, when the sun was just starting to rise, we were patrolling behind the lines over France when we suddenly saw a convoy of trucks. As we got closer, we found they were Red Cross. They were actually ambulances, but the ambulances—there must have been 40 of them—were led at the front and trailed at the back by troop carriers. It seemed strange to see a convoy like that led by a half-track.

F/L Sid Bregman and his Spitfire IX, 9G-Q Queenie (MJ 627), 441 Squadron. Bregman left the invasion stripes on the underwing and fuselage until October 1944. – Sid Bregman

THE JET JOB

J.J. Boyle, D.F.C., 411 Squadron

LATE in 1944, the Luftwaffe introduced the first operational jet aircraft of the war, the Me 262 twin-engine fighter. With a top speed in excess of 500 miles an hour, it could quickly outdistance the Spitfire IX, and since the Germans' main tactic seemed to be to attack from above out of the sun, we felt quite defenceless against them. With so much speed, their one passing attack would take only seconds, and since it was so difficult to spot them right at the outset, we always felt exposed and vulnerable.

On December 23, we were bounced by a lone Me 262. He was on us before the first warning shout came through my earphones. Luckily, his fire missed everyone. As he sped past us, he came right into my gunsight and I fired a cannon burst instinctively. I saw a flash on his rudder that looked like an explosive cannon strike but it could just as easily have been a sun flash. He raced away from us and was gone in seconds. After we landed, my No. 2 confirmed he had seen an explosion on the rudder. As a result of our ops report, I received credit for one damaged enemy aircraft. I took quite a razzing from my squadron mates about "seeing things" because none of us really had thought we could hit a jet. That was the first time I had seen an Me 262, and just the sight of it was exciting. Two days later I saw my second one.

On Christmas morning, our entire wing received orders to provide maximum air support in the American sector to the south, where the Germans had broken through our lines in what came to be known as the Battle of the Bulge. Excitement was running high as we were briefed on the extensive German fighter activity around Bastogne and told that our entire wing—five squadrons—would be taking off within the hour.

Our squadron was the last to take off, and it wasn't long before we could hear the R.T. chatter of those way up ahead reporting enemy aircraft sightings. Our sense of anticipation grew by leaps and bounds. In the midst of this,

Jack Boyle, in DB-R (RR 201), named Sweet Sue V *after his baby daughter, 1945.* – Jack Boyle

A German Me 262, W/Nr. 500200, "X" of 2/KG 51. The aircraft was captured at Fassberg in 1945 and ended up in an Australian museum. The tip of rudder and tip of nose were painted red. – Cecil Mann

I couldn't believe my ears when I heard the voice of my new No. 2 calling to report a ropy engine that was running so rough he thought he shouldn't go on. Since a lame aircraft was never permitted to go home alone, this meant I would have to escort him back to base and miss out on all the activity just ahead of us. At first there was some doubt in my mind about the seriousness of the engine problem as this was the very first operational trip of my No. 2. An "early return" was usually examined for validity, to detect any sign of inordinate combat nervousness. I decided we couldn't risk going on and reported to the C.O. that we were breaking off and heading for home. I was sorely disappointed by this turn of events, and grumbled to myself all the way home about bad luck and fickle fate.

As we neared home base at Heesch, we were far too high, and to get rid of the excess height, I stuck the nose almost straight down in a screaming spiral dive. As my speed shot past 500 miles an hour, out of nowhere appeared an Me 262, flown by Oblt. Lamle of 1/KG51. It took only a second to see to my gun sight and safety catch and then I was right behind him. My first burst of cannon fire hit his port engine pod, which began streaming dense smoke. He immediately dove for the deck as an evasive tactic, but with only one engine he couldn't outrun me. I scored several more hits before he clipped some tall treetops and then hit the ground at an almost flat angle. His aircraft disintegrated in stages from nose to tail as it ripped up the turf for several hundred yards until only the tail assembly was left. It went cartwheeling along just below me at about my speed. Fire and smoke marked his trail. As I circled, Dutch farmers emerged from their barns and waved up at me.

In the few minutes it took to return to base, I thought about how fast the whole thing had happened and realized I was now more excited than I had been during the actual attack. Upon landing and pulling into my usual slot, my mechanics were waiting for me, almost jumping up and down in their welcome. When I had dismounted, the armourer came up and said he always wondered when he was reloading my guns what the circumstances must have been when I fired them, and what a thrill it had been for him to have actually seen his guns shooting down an enemy aircraft. As a matter of fact, most of the airmen in the entire wing had witnessed the whole attack. Because it was noon on Christmas Day, they had all been lined up for turkey dinner. At the sound of gunfire they had hit the deck, facing up in case there was anything to see. On this day it was an Me 262 with a Spit right on its tail. Later, everyone told me what a thrilling spectacle it had been for them. For me too.

CHRISTMAS EVE, 1944

John Patus, 416 Squadron

I don't recall a lot of my war experience, owing to a violent crash landing. I was in 416 City of Oshawa Squadron. On Christmas Eve, 1944, we were on a patrol. I was flying SM 228. We ran into some light flak. Apparently, I was one of several hit.

I made a crash landing into a rocky field at very high speed—maybe 300 miles an hour. As I had little or no control, my Spitfire broke into pieces. Only the cockpit section remained, with me inside.

I was left dazed, bleeding, and half-dead, hanging nearly upside down. I would have died except that a few days later, a curious American G.I. poked around in the wreckage and found me. He was very surprised, as so little remained of my aircraft.

I was badly injured, and being left untended and unnoticed for days did not help. Thus, my memories of this and of some other events in my life I would like to recall are sketchy or non-existent.

It was a bad way to spend Christmas, although I really liked flying and enjoyed the companionship and camaraderie of those days. One of the fellows I trained with, Bill Clifford, went on to fly Typhoons, and my other friend, Chuck Darrow, flew Spits, also in the 416. We still keep in touch.

I have a few photographs and mementos of those days, though now it is hard to believe it all happened, especially in my case where recall is hard or impossible. Yet there I am in the photos, so it must be true.

F/L R.D. "Dagwood" Phillip, 416 Squadron, surveyed the damage done to his Spitfire XVI, DN-P (SM 311), on December 24, 1944, when several 416 Squadron Spitfires were hit by flak. "Still shaking, eh, Dag?" – DND PL 41349

Recollections

G.D. Cameron, D.F.C., 401, 402 Squadrons

I completed my first operations tour with 402 Squadron, out of Kenley and Redhill in 11 Group. There, we flew the Spitfire V and later the Spitfire IX. In October 1942, I moved to Malta to serve with 249 Squadron, RAF. There, we flew Spit Vs. By general consensus, the aircraft on Malta were all "clapped out." It was not uncommon to fly an aircraft that had a bullet hole in the propeller blade. The hole would have been well sanded, thus allowing the prop to be balanced. After Malta, I returned to England and completed the usual tour of instructing at Eshott in Northumberland.

I returned to Canada in November 1943 for a month's leave. Unfortunately, I was stuck here for ten months flying the Hurricane II. I was categorized as supernumerary for instructional purposes. In short, I was to give instruction to Canadian Home War Fighter Squadron No. 129 on the tactics of wartime flying. There were indeed some very good pilots. Generally, it was a very good flying club.

The Hurricane was a marvellous aircraft with a wide undercarriage and very few vices. I got into the bad habit of making wheel landings, because the runways were so long and it would have taken too long to taxi to our squad hangar. Needless to say, the aerodromes in England for fighter aircraft use had short runways. When I say runways, this could mean grass or asphalt or, later, interlocking metal strips.

I commenced my second tour by joining 401 Squadron a few miles from Brussels, Belgium. We then moved up as the war proceeded and were ultimately at Heesch, Holland, for the winter of 1944–45.

It was on the morning of January 1, 1945, that German fighters launched a massive raid. I understand that they were attempting to strike all Allied fighter airfields to destroy our aircraft. No doubt the Germans expected that we would not be prepared on New Year's morning and would probably be suffering from hangovers. I imagine that a good many Allied pilots were in such a condition.

My part in this particular episode was as leader of Yellow Section. I was flying MJ 448 that day. We were all seated in our aircraft on the taxi strip awaiting takeoff. Red Section, for some reason, had been delayed on taking off. As I glanced up to the general northeast, I saw a large wave of enemy aircraft at a height of about 100 feet. It seemed to me that they were sure to see our fighter strip and strafe us. I was thinking, "Am I better off to duck behind my bulletproof windshield or to try to swing my aircraft around and duck behind the bulletproof shield behind the pilot's seat?"

In fact, I did neither. I called on the radio and told Red Section to get the hell off the ground. There were about 50-plus enemy above the drome. The Red Section then took off, and I scooted out to follow them. We were flying off a metal-strip runway that was quite short. Naturally, I got off the ground as quickly as possible. Once airborne, I screwed my rudder so that I would be flying somewhat sideways, thus destroying the lines of sight of any aircraft attempting to shoot me down.

Apparently, the enemy aircraft saw the fighter strip at the last minute and shot a few rounds into it. I reached 1,000 feet in a very short time. I glanced down and saw two 109s in echelon to the right at perhaps 100 to 200 feet. They were apparently following the main body of German fighters. Somehow they had been left behind.

I was at an angle of approximately one-quarter to the right of each. I lowered the nose and fired a short burst of cannon and machine-gun fire and struck the right aircraft immediately to the rear of the cockpit. There was a brilliant flash as though I had struck the oxygen tank. The aircraft then dropped down, hit the ground and blew up. I took a similar shot at the leading aircraft of the two and hit

G.D. "Cam" Cameron with a Spitfire V from 402 Squadron. – G.D. Cameron

him at about the same point on his aircraft. It too burst into a flash and struck the ground almost immediately.

I had, of course, been looking around, and away to my right saw another 109 approximately 1,000 yards away. All was clear on my tail, so I gave my attention to the third aircraft. I lined up my sight and raised the dot to allow for the drop at such a long distance. I hit this aircraft in the engine with a burst. When it turned port and headed toward me, I gained height for the advance and what I expected to be a first-class dogfight. A damaged enemy aircraft was still dangerous. The pilot of such a craft would continue to attempt to destroy Allied aircraft as long as he could.

It is difficult to say whether this pilot was green (the Luftwaffe was short of experienced pilots) or whether a further battle would have been hopeless because I had inflicted too much damage. Whatever the case, he started heading for home. I sat on his tail for perhaps five miles and emptied my entire ammunition load into his aircraft. There was no attempt by him to take evasive action—he just seemed to be flying straight and level with throttle wide open. I pulled to his right and flew formation with him and saw him slumped over. I thought about how silly my position was as I was now a target for any aircraft behind me.

I soon broke to the right, continuing to observe him and my own tail. This aircraft eventually lost altitude and skidded into a field on its belly. I returned to the aerodrome to refuel and rearm. Though I wanted to become airborne immediately, I was ordered to report to Intelligence and relate the incident and details of my flight. I later jumped in a jeep and tried to locate the aircraft and thus obtain a personal trophy. I was unable to locate it.

On later flights, I destroyed another aircraft and also recorded a probable. Thus, my total score claimed is five destroyed, three probables, and two damaged. I have seen a record crediting me with five and one half aircraft destroyed.

Many writers have referred to the "Beautiful Spitfire," and I couldn't agree more. As I have said so often in the past, the Spit is so like a lovely woman—beautiful but deadly.

Living on the Edge

Cecil Mann, ground crew, 401 Squadron

On New Year's Day, 1945, at a temporary airfield at Heesch in Holland, the morning was clear and cold.

Squadron 411, our sister squadron on the field, had taken off on a bombing mission into Germany earlier that morning and should have been returning soon. It was nearing 8 a.m.

The roar of aircraft motors filled the air. Looking up, we discovered they were not ours but were German FWs and 109s. Coming in low, bearing across the airfield, they began firing their machine guns and cannons, systematically strafing the field. At that precise moment, 411 Squadron returned and immediately attacked our attackers, sweeping in on them from the rear, creating a rift in their strafing.

The remainder of our planes on the ground, those that were still serviceable, had already been loaded with 500-pound bombs. Those bombs slowed our Spitfires down during takeoff and made them much more vulnerable to the enemy. They also cut down on manoeuvrability in the air. So they had to be removed before takeoff. To remove a bomb from a Spitfire takes about three minutes, two men, and a cart similar to a wheelbarrow but with two wheels on one end. This is pushed under the plane from the front and raised to cradle the bomb, which is then released and wheeled away.

Ground crews, fitters, riggers, and armourers rushed to the planes—the fitters to start the motors, the riggers to strap the pilots in, and the armourers to remove the bombs. All this while we were under fire from 41 German fighters.

Unfortunately, no Spitfire could start its motor until its bomb had been removed because the cart and armourer had to pass under the propeller area to remove the bomb, which hung

Cecil "Smokey" Mann atop YO-A, F/L Sheppard's kite, with artwork in progress. Note the early design of the windscreen. – Cecil Mann

441 Squadron air-to-air photo of a Spitfire IX (MA 422) flown by F/O J.A. McIntosh on April 18, 1945, on Ramrod 1544 in a daylight escort for Lancasters. – R.H. Walker, S. Bregman

in the centre of the plane under the pilot's seat.

The RAF manual stated that a bomb that was already armed with a detonator could not be removed from the plane or it would explode. After all, this was their purpose.

Having worked with explosives for four years, and having taken every course available, I understood them inside and out.

The distance from the bomb to the ground under a parked Spitfire was no more than 20 inches. These particular bombs were fused in the nose. When dropped from a high altitude, the nose, being heavier, dropped faster. The bomb came down perpendicular so that its nose struck the ground first, which drove the firing pin into the detonator, causing it to explode, which, in turn, ignited the powder in the main chamber exploding the bomb. However, with only 20 inches to fall, there was neither time nor space for the nose to tilt down sufficiently to strike the ground before the belly of the bomb did; therefore, it would merely land on its belly and lie there without exploding. Even so, the RAF manual stated that bombs with detonators installed must not be dropped.

That morning, time was of the essence. The fitter was ready and waiting, the rigger was strapping the pilot into the cockpit seat, and the German planes were spraying bullets all over the field. I threw caution to the wind and, standing on the wing, reached into the cockpit, past the pilot, and pressed the electric bomb-release button. There was a dull thud as the bomb hit the ground. The pilot's face turned pale as he stared at my thumb on the button. There was no explosion. The fitter started the motor, and the rigger and I swung the tail of the plane sideways manually so it would miss the bomb as the plane pulled away from the parking area to take off, which it did unencumbered by its previous load. It was the first plane off the field and into the air.

The dogfight lasted about half an hour before the remaining German planes left hurriedly for home. Our pilots had done well. Of the 41 German planes that attacked us, only 17 flew away toward Germany. Our score was 27 kills—two of them to my pilot.

Later that day, when things had returned to near normal, my pilot looked me up in the armament area. He was grinning with his success, and he said to me, "This morning when you pushed that bomb-release button, I thought you had blown us all up. Why didn't it explode?"

All I could say was that I didn't believe it would. The RAF may not have agreed, but we were still alive.

411 Squadron, December 1944.
Front row: McConnell, Olsen, Boyle, (F/C B Flight), Panchuck (with glasses), Garr, Gilberstad, MacAulay, C.O. Newell.
Middle row: Pryde, Gardiner, Wilson, Young, Campbell, Ustinov, Graham, McCracken, Servos (Adj).
Back row: Thomson, Audet, MacDonnell, McNeice, Ireland, (F/C A Flight), Cooke.
Top: Harrison and Stewart. – RCAF, Jack Boyle

Outfoxed

J.J. Boyle, 411 Squadron

THURSDAY January 4, 1945, promised to be another good day. Again we were assigned to sweeps, our favourite op, and it was a lovely bright morning. The 411 took off and headed first for the airfields the Germans were using around Hengelo. Dick Audet was sub-leader of Red Section, in the right-hand figure four of our formation. We were all very proud as we could be of Dick, who had shot down five enemy aircraft in one encounter the previous Friday. He had borrowed my aircraft, *Sweet Sue V*, for that flight, and I was proud of her too.

As we flew over Hengelo at about 10,000 feet, the squadron was ordered to spread out and individually carry out evasive action, which we called weaving, as a defensive measure against flak. Unfortunately, our concentration on these weaving manoeuvres led to a breakdown in our visual cross-cover protection. The word "break!" was screamed through our earphones. Immediately everyone broke 180 degrees hard to port, just in the nick of time, as we would have been sitting ducks for the FW 190s that had just bounced us. Before I knew it, a 190 came into my gunsight. My first cannon burst struck his cockpit area. With my throttle on full, I was overtaking him too quickly. The 190 had become listless and was making no effort to take evasive action. I cut my throttle and put my wing down in a radical slip to lose speed, as I was now right above him. I could see the pilot slumped forward with his chute straps clearly visible over his shoulders, and ragged damage around the cockpit.

Breaking off, I was amazed that I couldn't see another aircraft in the sky except for a distant dot. I took after it and before long recognized it as another 190. I tried to stay below the line of sight he would have in his rearview mirror. After what seemed like an eternity, I had closed to about 500 yards before he spotted me and a wild chase began. He tried a series of tight, high-speed turns, and each time I was able to make up some distance on him. Beginning at 250 yards, I fired a short burst every time I could line him up in my sights. I hit him once on a wingtip, and again on the tip of his rudder, but damage was slight. In the final turn, with just about all the G force I could stand, I hit him once again on a wingtip and he flipped wildly out of control and fell straight down.

I confidently watched him go, expecting to see him crash and explode. Instead he pulled

Dick Audet became an ace on December 29, 1944, when he shot down five enemy fighters in one day. He was flying his friend Jack Boyle's aircraft, DB-G (RR 201), according to the logbook. In this photograph Audet is with his own aircraft, a Spitfire IX, DB-A (MK 950, coded R for a time), in which he was killed while strafing locomotives on March 3, 1945. – DND PL 41719, Steve Sauvé

out of the dive and began climbing back up to meet me. I can't describe how foolish I felt, having fallen for such a simple trick. I had lost all my tactical advantage, and within seconds we would be even-steven in a head-on attack.

Just then another Spit appeared from above and made a vertical passing attack. My quarry was diverted enough that I could get right on his tail, and as he dove for the deck, my fire blew chunks off him all the way down. I was so ashamed and unnerved, I continued to fire longer than I knew was necessary and didn't let up until he crashed and exploded.

Back in the ops room, while we were making out our combat reports, Dick Audet came in and asked, "Which one of you guys made a head-on attack on a 190, because I hit him in my attack."

I was only too happy to settle for a score of one-half on that one, because without Dick's help, God only knows what might have been the outcome. We learned later that seven 190s had bounced us and that we had destroyed six of them without suffering any losses ourselves, except for my self-esteem.

Chuck Darrow from Toronto, in a 416 Squadron Spitfire XVI, DN-A (TA 739), with a conventional cockpit canopy, April 1945. Darrow was later one of the first to fly a Spitfire XVI (TB 891) with a bubble canopy. He preferred the improved vision. – Charles Darrow

RECOLLECTIONS

Chuck Darrow, 416 Squadron

I flew a Spitfire IX and Spitfire XVI in 416 Squadron in the latter part of the war. Mainly, our duties consisted of ground attack—trains and road transport.

The XVI was similar to the IX except that it had a Packard Merlin, which was not considered as reliable as the Rolls-Royce Merlin, and the rumour was that the engines we got were those rejected by Bomber Command. It was just a joke, of course, but we did have some losses. Also, the Spitfires we flew had clipped wings, which caused some pilots trouble at first, when they were not used to them.

One fellow, after returning from leave, nearly flew the aircraft into a train because he was not used to the clipped wings. They gave the Spitfire a different feel and were supposed to improve our roll rate among other things. The overall difference was relatively minor, and to me they did not look as nice as the full wing.

We did not see much of the Luftwaffe in the air. We mainly saw flak. I was glad I did not have to take to my parachute, as I found that someone had removed it and replaced it with some blankets. I don't know how long I had been flying that way—maybe three or so missions. Silk was in demand on the black market for ladies' stockings. Apart from the shock of this discovery, my biggest dismay at the time was that I was going to have to pay for it. We were responsible for our equipment, even if it was stolen. However, I was able to claim it as one of the casualties of the sudden and unexpected raid by the Luftwaffe on New Year's morning, 1945.

We did not see much more of the Luftwaffe until the end of the war, when we saw a lot of German planes on the ground, on the airfields we captured. I took to flying a captured Bucker 181, a light aircraft, on a few flights. Some wires came up and hit me while I was doing some low flying, and that put me out of action for a while.

My aircraft in 416 was usually coded DN-A, and I flew a Mark XVI with that code for a long time (TA 739). My favourite aircraft was the Mark XVI with the bubble hood, which I thought was a big improvement over the old style, as you could see around much better. I flew one of the first ones in 416.

After the war, I also flew the Mark XIV on occupation duties with 416 Squadron, and then the new jets. I always thought the Spitfire was a beautiful aircraft.

"Johnnie" Johnson's Beer

Brian "Blackie" MacConnell, 402 Squadron

I flew Hurricanes in 129 Squadron in Canada for some time, and then in 1944 I was sent overseas. I flew various marks of Spitfire. I had heard of the new Spitfire XIVs and had asked for them when I was at OTU.

I was posted to 402 Squadron, which was the first RCAF squadron equipped with Mark XIVs. I landed, with three or four other pilots, at Brussels in an Anson. Our kit was taken out of the aircraft and put on the ground, and we were standing around. Another pilot (I think his name was Riddell) and I were waiting for a lift to the squadron, and I noticed a barrel of beer among the kit we carried. I very carefully moved my kit aside and worked it over toward the barrel.

Then a truck came and a sergeant asked, "You're for 126 Wing?" We said, "Yes." He said, "Fine, where's your kit?" We pointed to the barrel and our kit bags, and the beer went into the truck.

When the truck arrived at Diest, I met the adjutant of the 402, Alex Cronsberry. During our first discussion, I mentioned that I came from Lindsay, Ontario. He said, "Oh, that's where Ken Sleep is from." Sleep was the F/L in charge of A Flight, and Alex said, "We'll put you in his flight." When I was talking with Sleep, I asked him, "What should I do with the beer?" He said, "What beer?" and I said, "I brought a barrel of beer!" He said, "Real English beer?" I said, "Yes."

It was only later on, while we were enjoying the beer—now hidden in Sleep's room, since we did not want to share it with the other squadrons—that I noticed on the end of the barrel, written in chalk: J. Johnson—127 Wing. The only J. Johnson at 127 Wing was of course, the very well-known Johnnie Johnson. So if I ever meet Johnnie, I will have to thank him for the beer.

Brian "Blackie" MacConnell of 402 Squadron flew this Spitfire XIV, AE-B Emily (NH 703), in the spring of 1945. Earlier it had been the exclusive aircraft of Ernie Mouland. Photo taken in Heesch, the Netherlands. – Rick Richards

Shooting Down a Jet Bomber

Brian "Blackie" MacConnell, 402 Squadron

I never did get a D.F.C. or anything close to it, mainly because you got those for shooting down aircraft, and when I was in the squadron, it was late in the war, and we rarely saw any German aircraft. We spent most of our time shooting up trucks and trains, or dive-bombing rail lines, in support of the army.

In the 402 we flew the new and more powerful Spitfire XIV, with the Griffon engine. My usual aircraft was AE-B (NH 703), with my future wife's name, Emily, on the nose. However, on April 19, 1945, I was flying AE-J (RN 119), as my usual aircraft was in for service. I remember that we were flying in battle formation at about 10,000 feet in a northwest direction over Germany, on an armed recce near Rheine.

We were just looking for something to do, when I noticed a shadow moving along the ground in basically the same direction we were going. I followed it up toward the sun and noticed a single aircraft, fairly close to the ground, at about 1,000 feet. Not knowing what it was, I broke from the formation. After I got far enough away that I knew I would be the first one there, I called back to get them to cover me. I dived down and pulled in behind it.

I didn't recognize what it was. For several moments I was in an ideal position to fire, but I held off. I thought I should hold my fire until I was sure what it was. It was a twin-engine aircraft with a single fin and rudder. I pulled out beside it to see if it might be an American aircraft such as a B-26 variant, or some other type I could not identify. It seemed likely it was one of the new jets, and I didn't want to be like a fellow I had heard of who had shot up an RAF Meteor jet, thinking he had an Me 262.

But I saw that there was a big cross on the fuselage, so I guess I said to myself, "It's one of them." I got back in behind it and gave a short burst. One of the engines started smoking and a few flames came out, and it started in a low turn—a controlled turn—and I followed it

Brian "Blackie" MacConnell – Brian MacConnell

down. I stopped shooting, because obviously it was going down. Then it headed for an open field, and just before it crash-landed, I was sure I could see somebody trying to get out. A parachute caught on the tail, but I later learned it could have been a drogue chute to slow the plane down—a new idea then.

Anyway, I caught all this on cinecamera film, just to prove that I at least got one, and then went back to base with the squadron. When I landed, they could tell that I had fired my guns, and at debriefing, they asked me what it was, and I had to think, "What was it?" It was a single-tail twin-engine, and I couldn't think of anything but a Ju 88, so I said, "a Ju 88," and that was the end of that.

I went on leave for a short while after that. When I came back, the war must have been over. Chunkie Gordon, the squadron leader, said "Blackie, you stupid"—that was his favourite expression—and then told me I'd shot down an Arado 234—a German jet bomber. How I was supposed to know, I couldn't say, as we were given no information at all on this type. Nothing in our aircraft recognition. Had I known, I would have opened up sooner, as he could have got away.

The intelligence people told me that the likeliest reason I caught up to him was that he was on a landing approach. We were probably near the airfield. On the same mission, the same day, the airfield defences had shot down Cowan, who was believed to be chasing another Arado in his Spitfire (RM 727).

[German records show the loss of a Major Polletien (operations officer of KG 76), who was shot down by "RAF" fighters as he returned to his base at Lübeck Blankensee, following an operation in the Breda area. The Rheine area is more or less on the direct flight path between Breda and Lübeck. So it seems very likely that this was the aircraft downed by MacConnell.]

If we had been provided with some information on this aircraft, it might have helped. At the time, we had only the most rudimentary information on the German jets—a little on the Me 262 but nothing but rumours about the others.

Unfortunately, with the war over, there's no interest in changing the records, so it has stayed in the records as a Ju 88. I guess a thousand guys shot one of those down, but not many shot down 234s.

We saw 262s—the other jet—a few times. When we were flying along in battle formation, we'd see a speck in the sky coming toward us from the front, and it would fly straight at us, maybe take a shot at something, and then it would go screaming through us, and we'd all turn to try to get a shot at it, but by then it was long gone—and then it would take us 15 minutes to re-form!

When we took over Fassberg, there were any number of German jets on the airfield there, including the little Me 163 rocket plane that landed on skids. We could sit in the cockpit of the Me 262 and some of the other jets we saw, and just marvel, although even we did not appreciate what the new jets were all about or what a change they would bring about in future aircraft design.

I flew the magnificent Spitfire XIV for the rest of my time with 402 Squadron. I was given a new one—a bubble-canopy version, still coded AE-B (SM 884)—which I flew in May and June 1945. However, the war had indeed ended, after 93.25 hours of ops for me. I volunteered to fight in Japan but was soon sent home.

The type of aircraft shot down by "Blackie" MacConnell on April 19, 1945. A twin-jet Arado 234 used for bombing and reconnaissance by the Luftwaffe in 1944 and 1945. The aircraft shown is from KG 76 (140356), the same unit as the one downed. – IWM MH 4871

DIVE-BOMBING

Bill Harper, 421 Squadron

My most unforgettable moment happened on April 12, 1945. We were located at B100 Airfield at Goch, just inside the German border near Kleve.

My second trip that day was another jaunt to the Oldenburg area about 175 miles northeast of us. The last few days we had flown several armed recces and strafed any ground targets we discovered. This trip was a squadron "dive-bombing do" against Oldenburg's railway marshalling yards.

Each of us carried a 500-pound bomb under the belly of our Spitfire. Using our gunsight as a bomb sight, we dove almost vertically from about 10,000 feet. A couple of seconds after we initiated pull-out at about 2,000 feet, we released the bomb. Then we corkscrewed up and away to avoid flak.

As usual on this kind of trip, I fired my cannons and machine guns during the dive. My theory was that this would encourage the Jerry gunners to keep their heads down.

Only seconds after releasing my bomb, I heard and felt a loud explosion and everything seemed to go dead. In reality, a 40 mm A.A. shell had entered my starboard wing root (just missing the radiator), passed by my right heel, and travelled up and behind my back and out the left side of the fuselage. It left a jagged six-inch hole just behind my coupe top, where it had exited.

The dead sensation was caused by the shell knocking out my electrical system. The usually noisy radio was quiet. Then it dawned on me that the Merlin was still running smoothly. My first reaction after counting arms and legs was to pour the coal and start climbing.

By the time I realized I had survived and that my engine was running fine, I was at 25,000 feet, completely alone, the only aircraft in the sky in hostile territory over Germany.

Without further ado, I stuck the nose down and headed for home as fast as I could.

F/L Bill Harper with his Spitfire XVI, AU-J Dorothy II *(TB 886), the second Spitfire he named after his wife.* – Bill Harper

I caught up to our squadron just as they tightened up their formation before peeling off for landing. With my radio dead, many hand-signs were directed at the hole in my fuselage, with me wiping my brow in reply.

A happy postscript to this adventure was that I got a replacement aircraft. The shell had holed a main longeron, which meant my original AU-J (SM 476) had to be written off. Eight days later, I received my new AU-J (TB 886), the first blister-hood or rearview fuselage Mark XVI in 127 Wing.

Many pilots coveted this aircraft, so before some C.O. appropriated it, I had Dorothy II painted on the side of the nose (the original Dorothy being Mrs. Harper). I believe *Dorothy II* was probably the most photographed Spitfire on our wing.

AU-T Lady Joan *(SM 392) was flown by Chuck Lyons in April 1945.* – Lloyd Burford and Bill Harper

Bill Harper's AU-J Dorothy II *(TB 886), named after his wife, was the first bubble-canopy Spitfire XVI in 127 Wing. April 1945.* – Bill Harper

Ground Attack

Lloyd Burford, 421 Squadron

IT was so late when I arrived in 421 Squadron that I never got to see the enemy in the air, but happily, I had a few air-to-ground attacks. I had average results, except for my last two, which I feel were quite good. I learned how fast an attack can turn, with the attacker ending up on the receiving end of anti-aircraft fire.

Late on May 2, 1945, I took off with a section of eight, flying Spitfire XVIs, on my third sortie that day (SM 359). The first had been aborted by ground fog, and our leader had trouble finding a field that was still open. It seemed we were the only ones still heading north; the other flights could be heard on the R.T. going back. We were finally told that Fassberg would be open for a few more minutes. We made for it and got in just before being socked right in. We flew back to Schneverdingen around noon. On our second sortie that day, late in the afternoon, we shot up a few trucks, destroying some. In the early evening, Danny Browne led eight of us on our third sortie. Bill Harper was on this flight too, probably leading Pink Section. My No. 1 called to the chief to report a couple of trucks below and he could have a go at them. Danny called back, "Okay, but stay away from the canal [Kiel], we'll wait for you."

My No. 1 led me out, and away we went with our attack. I dropped below my leader so I could see the target and waited for him to open fire. When he didn't, I opened fire, as the target was coming up fast. My first shots hit right in front of the truck, the next ones dead centre, and then the target exploded. In the meantime, my leader had pulled up hard to the right and I chased up after him. As I approached him, he stalled it over on the left wing and went straight down on the second truck. In very short order, I was attacking from a very low altitude and getting a lot of flak back. The

W/C Stan Turner's Spitfire (TB 300) was a very personal Spitfire. Turner had his initials painted boldly in white and the inner, white areas of the roundels enlarged. The clipped wings were later replaced with regular rounded wingtips. – R.H. Beall

Richard "Hap" Beall's last Spitfire, AU-H Panama Bound (SM 309). Richard was one of many RCAF pilots with roots in other parts of the world. Today, at Rockcliffe, Ottawa, the National Aviation Museum Spitfire is painted as AU-H. – Bill Harper

second truck blew up with a large flash and we found ourselves right over the canal.

What happened in the next 60 seconds or so was unbelievable to me, being very inexperienced. Everything in the area opened up on us, and I used every skid and slip trick I could think of. I swear I must have bent the throttle trying to get a little more out of that Spit. We were very lucky and made our escape unharmed. We tried to approach a couple of other Spit flights, but they took evasive action, so we hightailed it for home.

The ground crew showed me a small hole in the prop of the aircraft I was flying, as though a single small-calibre shell had gone through it.

On another flight we were on our way home from a sortie when the forward control officer called to say he had an unidentified group of aircraft on his radar. He gave our leader a heading and gave us a break port and we were heading their way. There were a few layers of cloud, and control gave us a course and let down to about 9,000 feet. Control called that we should see them below us at about ten o'clock as we broke through the bottom cloud.

By this time, we had good speed. When we cleared the cloud, there they were—eight of them and eight of us. What a sight. My heart was pumping pretty good, as I hadn't seen an enemy in the air before.

Our No. 1 took the leader, and I took the next. They were in battle formation for us, one apiece. We were in to about 400 yards when our leader called for us to pull off, that they were Typhoons. We were so close over them when we went by that I think some of them may have needed a change of shorts. That was as close as I came to aerial combat.

C/O 127 Wing and ace pilot "Stocky" Edwards with his Spitfire JF-E (TD 147), May 1945. – J.F. Edwards

W/C Edwards in Schneverdingen, Germany, about 30 miles southwest of Hamburg, May 1945. – J.F. Edwards

A ground crew member sits atop Lloyd Burford's 421 Squadron aircraft, AU-V (TB 270), in 1945.
– Lloyd Burford

Canadian Spitfire pilots of 155 Squadron, Burma, April 1945. Their camp was not far from the Irrawaddy River. Left to right: F/O Doug Gillin, P/O Paul Ostrander, P/O May Russell, W/O G. Maclaine. The Spitfire VIII aircraft were donated by the Maharaja of Manjipur.

– RCAF, DND PL 60256, Paul Ostrander

THE LOST LEGION: CANADIANS IN THE RAF

Paul Ostrander, 155 Squadron RAF (Burma)

I flew the Spitfire Mark VIII in Burma. Conditions there were very primitive. Very hot, with little in the way of equipment. To change an engine, the ground crew would have to use a tree and a block and tackle. No special cranes.

I first soloed on June 25, 1942, in Fleet No. 4508 at No. 13 EFTS at St. Eugene, Ontario. Back then I flew a lot of Harvards, Masters, and DH 82s. I flew my first Spitfire, an early Mark II, in England in April 1943, at No. 61 OTU. I then did some flying in Algiers. In a Spitfire Vb (ER 680), I did a beat-up along with my friend Dobbs, flying a Hurricane out of the Setif airfield, which was full of Yanks and their Airacobras.

I flew Spitfires again at 2 TEU. These were very early model Mark I Spitfires that probably flew in the Battle of Britain. In May 1944 I was sent to India. I must have said something to upset someone, as it was commonly taken to be some sort of punishment to be shipped out there. If so, I don't know what I did. This suspicion was not much relieved when Ginger Lacey, the man who had shot down the bomber that bombed Buckingham Palace, was sent out to lead one of our Spitfire squadrons in India. The rumour was he had been too impatient with his commanding officers.

I started my flying with 155 Squadron in July 1944. The Spitfires—brand-new Mark VIIIs— had been paid for by the Maharaja of Manjipur. The Spitfire VIII had a retractable tail wheel and was a beautiful aircraft to fly. I always considered the Spitfire easy to fly, with none of the vices common to other aircraft. One thing I have never seen reported in any book is that the Spitfire VIII even gave us a stall warning. When approaching a stall, the wings would give a hammering noise. That was a big plus, and one that could save the life of a young, inexperienced fighter pilot.

Most of our flights were fairly routine. We escorted Hurricane fighter-bombers and C-47 Dakota transports doing their duties. On September 12, I escorted some Hurries to Kalewa. On landing, the tail-oleo of my Spitfire (DG-Z) collapsed on the runway. On October 6, 1944, we did a recce of the Pyingaing–Kalewa area to

A Spitfire VIII and pilots from 155 Squadron, Burma, April 1945. – Paul Ostrander

investigate an enemy force seen there. It turned out to be five tanks, which were finally identified as derelict British.

We did see some Japanese fighters—Oscars on occasion—but they were very elusive and I never caught any. We were faster but they were more manoeuvrable, and we hardly ever saw much of the enemy in the air. Mainly we flew against ground targets. On our rhubarbs and other missions, there could be bags of flak. The 17 Squadron seemed to have more luck finding Oscars.

The weather was awful at times. The monsoons brought rain, and visibility was often poor. On one flight, we were bringing in three Spitfires to our unit. Visibility was so bad that we finally ran out of gas and had to land in a small clearing. It was so small that we could not fly out again, and the aircraft were just left in the jungle. I read recently of some aircraft that were brought out of India by an aircraft enthusiast, and wonder if they were the ones we had left.

Owing to the primitive conditions, we took to wearing clothing that we had managed to collect in various places. It became a matter of personal taste, and we exhibited a wide variety of styles.

We must have seemed a wild and woolly lot both in appearance and flying style to the young squadron leader who was sent out to teach us some discipline. He wanted us to land in formation, in groups of three, with the next flight following right on our tail. This meant the group landing had to get out of the way right away. One time, our new S/L forgot where he was. When he landed, he just stopped. The following aircraft pulled up to miss him. He rolled one wheel from his undercarriage right over the coupe top of the startled S/L. The poor fellow didn't really fit in and was sent home soon after.

Our Spitfires were kept in good condition by our hard-working ground crew. We enjoyed flying low, and though we sometimes killed more jungle than enemy forces, we did lose a number of friends in the intense ground fire. I admired the courage of the C-47 transport drivers, who flew in low to drop supplies to the long-suffering ground troops.

I flew with 155 Squadron until May 31, 1945. Ginger Lacey often flew with us and did much to raise morale, as he was very well liked. I greatly missed the many friends I made during the war, and was pleased to keep in contact with some via reunions and in business.

"Blackie" MacConnell and his newer Spitfire XIV (SM 884), near the end of the war. – Brian MacConnell

The Last Day: Flying the Mark XIV Spitfire

Jack Rigby, 402 Squadron

I flew in the first RCAF squadron to be equipped with the Mark XIV Spitfire with the Griffon engine. It had a lot more power than the Mark IX or the Mark XVI. The greater power of the Griffon engine relative to the Merlin took some getting used to. Especially on landing.

Many pilots, especially those used to flying the Mark IXs, tried to come in to land at about 120 miles an hour. As a result, they tended to come in a bit heavy, as the nose of the Mark XIV was heavier than they were used to. They would begin to bounce, then panic and give it more power, getting into more trouble. They would hop and jump all the way down the strip. In fact, the way to do it was to come in at about 100 miles an hour. There was a lot of power in that engine, and one could control one's approach—I often landed at only 60 miles an hour.

I started out flying the Mark V and had only the most rudimentary instruction on the Mark XIV—one fellow just took me over to the airplane and pointed out all the tits and dials, pointing out those that were special to the XIV. While I always had a lot of respect for the airplane, I was never as afraid of it as others were.

One flight that did give me a scare occurred on May 4, 1945. There were 12 of us on a sweep into southern Denmark, mainly looking to shoot up truck convoys and the like. When we had completed our attacks, I was the last one out and had to hit the gas to catch up to the rest of the squadron. I was flying RM 933 coded AE-T that day.

I was going very fast when I caught up with the rest of the formation—over 400 miles an hour. I cut the throttle abruptly as I didn't want to overshoot them. The pitch control of the big five-bladed prop snapped back the angle of the blades as I slowed down abruptly. Just at that moment, a German Me 262 jet opened fire on me, getting strikes on my aircraft. I did not see him coming, and did not get a good look at him as I was too busy trying to regain control of my aircraft. I was down a long way before I did.

It was pure luck that he did not get me. I think I must have thrown off his aim when I slowed down so suddenly. I would have been very upset if he had killed me, as that would have meant dying on the last day of the war. As it turned out, that was the last operational flight of 402 Squadron.

We ended the war at a former German air base at Wunsdorf, which was so well camouflaged, particularly in the summer, that it was almost invisible under the trees and foliage. The only way I could find it was to line up on a fake runway, which was full of bomb craters, and then locate the actual runway! The camouflage was really that effective. Most of our runways at the time were made of metal strips. Landing on metal was a noisy affair.

Our final base was a far different affair, being a permanent Luftwaffe base with many amenities. The Germans had even enjoyed swimming pools and other facilities. We held a party there to celebrate V.E. Day, the end of the war in Europe. We brought in beer in the fuel-drop tanks of our Spitfires—in fact, we were already quite good at that. Finding women was a little more difficult, but we finally managed to round up all the nurses and WAAFs in the vicinity. As a reward for attending, we gave each of the women a medal. In fact, they were German medals, given to German women for having children. Anyway, they deserved a medal for the party we had!

I encountered few problems flying the Spitfire. Once, I was returning to base and had to

Ken Lawson, of 414 Squadron, flew this Spitfire XIV, "S" (MV 348), named Violet-Dorothy III *after his mother and his wife. April 1945.* – PA 95124, Ken Lawson

lose some height. I put the aircraft into a dive and was soon bending the needle at over 500 miles an hour. The aircraft did not fly properly at all and seemed to me to be behaving very strangely. I slowed down my dive, lost speed, and landed normally. I complained to the maintenance chief, who asked me how fast I was going. When I told him, he replied, "You clot, you were encountering compressibility!"

I had thought there was something wrong with the airplane, but in fact, he was right. It was then little understood, but speeds approaching that of sound cause a shock wave that interferes with the flying ability of aircraft.

I still love to fly, and have flown as much as I could since the war in many different aircraft. But to me, the Spitfire—especially the Mark XIV—was the ultimate.

Spitfires at Rockcliffe

Tom Percival *C.W. "Chuck" Doodson*

I flew Spitfire X4492 at Rockcliffe mainly for camera tests. It had a camera mounted in it that was synchronized with the gun button and gunsight. I flew it during the eclipse of the sun from Rivers, Manitoba, on July 9, 1945.

I am somewhat hazy on the details, but I believe it was about 4:30 a.m. The run was over the south end of Lake Winnipeg at around 27,000 feet. An Anson and a B-25 Mitchell also flew on the operation.

S/L Millman from the Royal Observatory (Ottawa or Montreal) was in charge. Millman was an astronomer; S/L Wiseman was in charge of the aircraft.

After returning to Ottawa, I went on B-25s for the balance of the year, mainly on photo flights. We also did photography in British Columbia and the Northwest Territories.

I did get some good pictures of the eclipse, and there were some published in *Life*, in a July or August issue.

My role in the RCAF was very modest. I became a flying instructor in England, in February 1942. On returning to Canada, I was attached to the Photo Survey Squadron at Rockcliffe, which was involved in mapping the Northwest Territories.

We used a variety of aircraft—Cansos, Ansons, B-25 Mitchells, Hurricanes, and Spitfires. My logbook and photos show Spitfire X4492, which I flew. While my recall is not as sharp as I would like it to be, I am pretty sure that the colours on the Spitfire were brown and green.

My most vivid recollection was of my first flight in the Spitfire—pure ecstasy. It was unbelievably smooth and responsive. It was so great I wanted to stay up there and fly forever!

Back to reality: the Spitfire was used for vertical-line overlaps from 20,000 feet. It was the first time some areas had ever been photographed accurately from the air.

A Spitfire V (X4555) at Rockcliffe, February 26, 1944. – PA 68006

When 421 Squadron was disbanded at the end of the war, Bill Harper went to 412 Squadron where he flew this Spitfire XIV, VZ-C, which had previously seen service with 402 Squadron as AE-C. – Bill Harper

443 Squadron Hornets on postwar duty. To the left is a Spitfire XIV, 2I-K, Doris, with a yellow and black spiral spinner, clipped wings, and bubble canopy. To the right is a Mark XVI, possibly 2I-S. – LAC Radio, Julien Shymko

The Occupation of Germany

Walter Thompson, 416 Squadron

IF you ask me about the Spitfire, I would have to say I don't think there was anything like it—for a propeller-driven airplane, it was really a thrill. In the Mark XIV version, with that Griffon engine, and five-bladed prop, it was quite a machine. In 416 Squadron I had my "own" Spitfire XIV, DN-N (SM 820), with my wife's name, Loie, painted on the nose.

During the occupation of Germany we did a fair amount of flying. Once in a while we would have mock air battles with U.S. Thunderbolts. There was an American airfield near the coast, and we used to meet them about halfway, at about 8,000 feet. One day, one of our lads collided with one of theirs—they both bailed out successfully, but there were two big bonfires on the ground! It was a dangerous game.

We had to have the ground crew ride on the tail to the takeoff point—you couldn't run up the Spitfires on the ground without somebody on the tail, and then you couldn't run them up at full power. We had to tie them to the ground for maintenance, to run them up to full power. There was a lot of torque—you applied full left rudder before you opened up the throttle, and then as you opened it, as you picked up speed, you eased up on the left, and by the time you were airborne, you had straightened out.

I had one memorable experience that scared the hell out of me. Spitfires were fitted with cartridge starters, and I think they had five cartridges on the revolver. This time, my ground crew only put two cartridges in, and we had a scramble. I pulled the lever to start, I fired one, and it didn't start. I fired the second one, and it didn't start. In the meantime, the rest of the squadron had taken off. Finally, the ground crew slapped in a couple more cartridges, and I got it going, so I was a way behind them when I took off.

I overboosted on the climb, and I just caught up to them, when I could smell something. It was a rank smell, like an electrical transformer when it's burning out. I had just pulled up in

Walter Thompson with his Spitfire XIV, DN-N Loie *(SM 820), 416 Squadron. Occupation forces, 1946.* – Walter Thompson

formation when one of the guys said, "Tommy, you're smoking!" By that time the whole cockpit had filled with smoke, and I started to get glycol and oil back.

What had happened was that when I overboosted, the engine then detonated, which blew a chunk out of the solar wall about the size of a silver dollar. It also cut the spark plug wires, which were all armoured. I held my altitude and was about 2,000 feet over the strip when I got back.

Steve Straub, another member of the squadron, was just then having engine trouble on his approach, so I had to wait and do an orbit and try to keep my altitude while Steve went in. Then I pulled in, and landed as close to the control van as I could, as fast as I could. (We didn't have a control tower, just a mobile van at the end of the runway.) Pink Face was the

A Spitfire XIV (TZ 198), with Tweetie Bird under the windscreen and, on the nose, Bugs Bunny in a beret carrying a newspaper. – Shymko, Knutson

A Spitfire XIV (RM 689), 443 Squadron, with a hornet on the nose, 1945. – Shymko, Knutson

controller's call sign, and he said he never saw anything like it. I was like a rat deserting a ship—as soon as I landed, I kicked left rudder, got off the runway and bailed out. The airplane was smoking to beat hell, and I thought it was going to blow up, but it didn't.

Other than flying Spitfires, we also did a bit of flying in our squadron on a captured Gruneau Baby II sailplane, which flew very well and was quite enjoyable. So after spending most of the war in training, and training others to fly, I finally saw a little bit of Europe.

A Spitfire IX, 401 Squadron, Wunsdorf, 1945, beside a Ju 88G of the Luftwaffe. – R. Finlayson

A Nightfighter Me 109G-10, white 44, with pale blue camouflage. In the background, a Spitfire XIV from 411 Squadron. – Bill Harper

The FW 190 flown by RCAF/RAF ace "Stocky" Edwards, JFE (933849). There is an Me 108 in the background with Stan Turner's initials on it. Note the bulged cockpit canopy. – Allan Bayly

Spitfires in Israel

Denny Wilson, 101 Squadron, IDF

I did most of my flying in the Second World War with 411 Squadron, RCAF, out of Holland in 1944.

After the war, I did some bush flying. While I was in Vancouver getting supplies (I was in a tailor's shop—this was back in the days when a crease in your pants was a necessity), a chance conversation led to my being recruited for Israel.

I am often asked why I went. It was a combination of things: I still had the flying bug, and it was a job. But also, I had seen the Bergen-Belsen concentration camp and it seemed to me that the State of Israel was the underdog.

Some of the time I spent in Israel 1948–49 was most interesting. I was a member of 101 Squadron, whose members included Canadians as well as other nationalities. Ezer Weizmann, now the President of Israel, was also a pilot in 101 Squadron.

We had three different kinds of aircraft: Spitfires, Mustangs, and Messerschmitts. I did not fly any particular Spitfire while in Israel—we flew what was available. My logbook tells me that the planes I flew during the 1948–49 war were a considerable mix, but more than half the time I flew Spitfires.

I had a friend I flew with by the name of Dick Dougherty, and we spent a lot of our time off the station together. When we had an afternoon off, we would take the bus to Tel Aviv, and whenever we needed a ride back to camp in Chatzor (the RAF called it Quatsina), we would pick out the handiest car available, cross the wires, and drive it back.

One day, the air force gave us a seven-passenger Chrysler, with a driver, for our own use, as long as we promised not to steal any more cars! On the first day, I drove over to Aquir

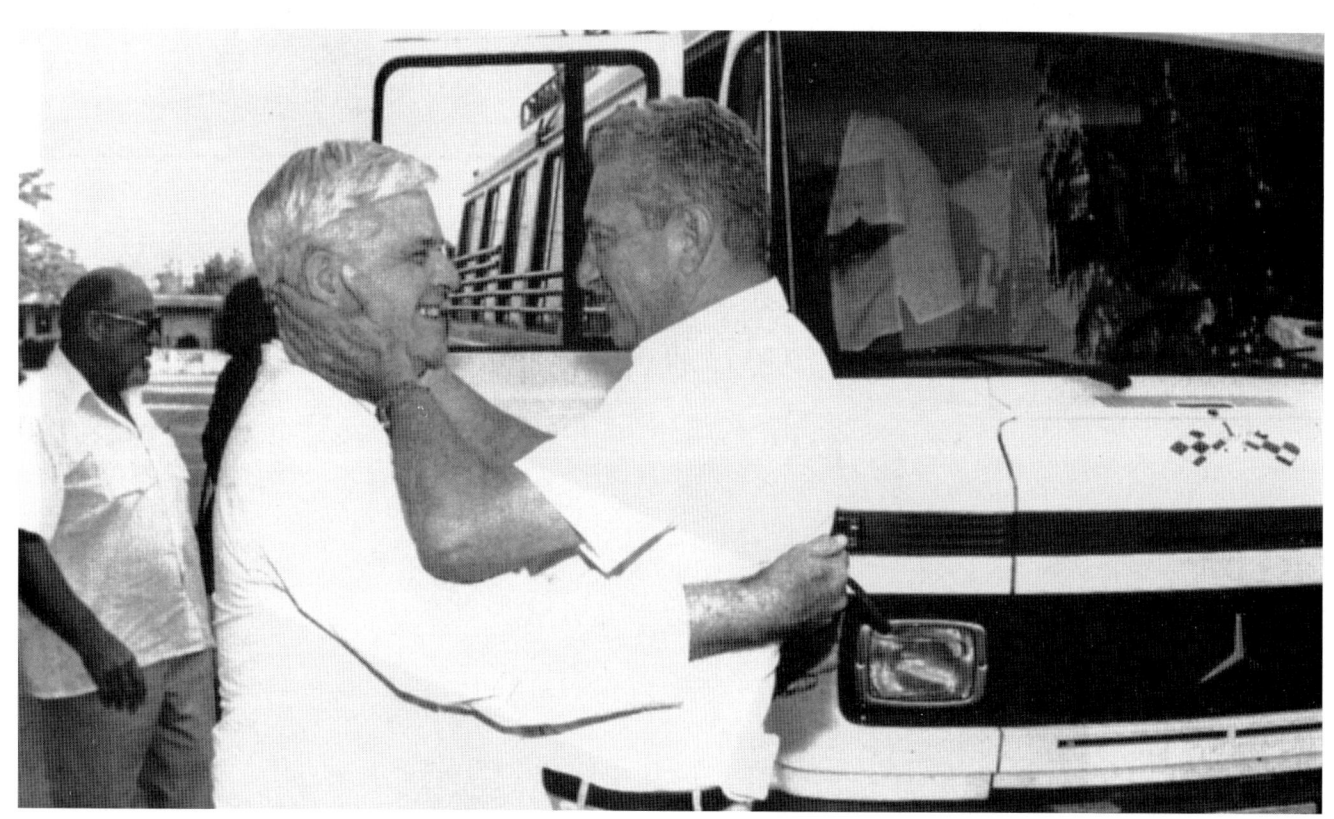

Ezer Weizman (right) greets Denny Wilson at an airport in Israel in 1986. – Denny Wilson

to visit Dick. When I got there, Dick took one look at me in the car with the private driver and asked, "Did you have any trouble stealing the driver?"

Christmas in Israel could have been just another day, but in 1948 the air force group got together and produced a Christmas dinner for all the Mahal pilots in 101 Squadron. We even had the turkey and trimmings, which was quite a surprise to us. After the dinner they took us by bus to the Christian church in Jaffa, where a service was held for all Christians. It was a very touching experience.

While I was flying a Spitfire over the Faluga Pocket on photo reconnaissance one day, our headquarters intercom picked up a conversation between an Egyptian pilot and his people on the ground. Apparently, he was flying supplies to his ground crew and, though I didn't know it, was carrying no ammunition. As I was flying without ammunition, it was a surprise to me that the Egyptian pilot panicked when he saw me, and promptly bailed out, making no effort to fire at me or elude me. Obviously he thought I was armed. What a way to get an aircraft! Not a shot was fired! I was credited with a destroyed.

The other two Egyptian planes I downed were legitimate kills, and I was credited for them. On December 31, 1948, while flying a Spitfire (2015) on a patrol over the Sinai, I spotted an Egyptian aircraft—an Italian Fiat (or Macchi)—coming back to its airfield at Bir Hama. He was below me, and I shot him down—the pilot bailed out.

On the way back, over Faluga, I caught an Egyptian Spitfire flying escort for a transport plane. The Spit started a tight turn, but I tightened with him. I used my machine guns only, as we were so short of ammunition that we'd been asked not to use our cannons. I made hits around his engine cowlings, and he spiralled down and blew up.

I left Israel in June 1949, finishing by training others to fly. When I visited in 1986, I was deeply impressed at what that country had become, and what that air force had become. Maybe we were responsible for some of it!

Flying the Last Spitfires

Guy Mott, D.F.C., Weapons Officer, D.F.C., 441, 18, 80 Squadrons

I flew the Spitfire in the Second World War in 441 Squadron, which was quite exciting, and I had many adventures. I wanted to remain in flying, and in 1947, the RAF came through recruiting air crew to go back to England. They had planned to take a considerable number of us back in, but they ended up taking only a hundred or so. They did the same thing in Australia, New Zealand, and South Africa. No one came from Australia—the Australian government stopped it—but when we recruits got over to England, we met up with South Africans, New Zealanders, and other Canadians.

When we first went over, there were about 50 in my group. We were put into one holding station, and we were there for quite some time. I got out in about two months to go to refresher flying school. I came back to that station about six months later on, and about half of them were still there waiting to go to refresher flying school. As time went on, we were all split up—you'd meet someone here or there—they were absorbed by the RAF.

Being in the RAF wasn't what I thought it would be. In peacetime, flying comes about last, and other duties become more important. To get any flying in, you had to go on flying courses, which I did. I took up the weapons side of it. We'd go on a course, and they'd teach us how the theory of air firing and the theory of bombing and gunnery worked in reality. When I came back, I had to leave the squadron for an OTU in Devon. Then I went back into Fighter Command, and joined a squadron where I flew Vampires and Spitfires. That was still in England.

A little over a year after I got there, I was posted to the Far East Air Force, to Singapore. There was an uprising in Malaya. I volunteered to go, but I didn't think I would because the other people in the flight were all RAF, and I thought they would be picked first, as I was the newest recruit there. And lo and behold, I was the one who went, because the other fellows didn't have the qualifications—they didn't have this, or they didn't have that. Taking all those courses paid off after all.

I flew out there on a BOAC Constellation, in civilian clothes, and arrived in Tenga Airport in Singapore. It was around January 5. I got posted to a new armament practice camp 300 or 400 miles north of Singapore, at a place called Butterworth, just across from an island called Penang.

They were starting up this new armament practice camp to train the squadrons there, because they were doing a lot of round strafing on these bandits they had in Malaya. I stayed there for almost a year. During that time I became the commanding officer of the armament practice camp.

By then the Communists had come rolling up to the boundaries of Hong Kong. This brings us up to the fall of 1949. I spent a year and a half posted in Hong Kong, as the weapons officer of the Kai Tak Wing. Kai Tak was the main aerodrome there. At that time we were flying Spit 18s and 24s. The last of the Spitfires!

They were a different aircraft from the Vs and IXs I had flown in the Second World War. They were powerful, with around 2400 horsepower. They had a five-bladed prop, longer oleo legs, stood up higher, and had a wing on them similar to a Mustang's. They could really go! They were powerful brutes, too, and the torque was terrific on takeoff. They had four cannons on them—short cannons that just protruded from the wings—but they'd pick up a thousand pounds of bombs, or eight rockets, plus these four guns. All the wheels were retractable including the tail wheel.

They had a longer range with extra gas tanks in the wings, and another 90-gallon tank right behind the pilot. It was quite an aircraft. The 18s were much like the wartime Mark XIV—they were nicely finished. But the 24s were the nicest, almost as well finished as photo reconnaissance Spitfires were. You could hardly

The powerful 2375 h.p. Rolls-Royce Griffon engine in a Spitfire XXIV (PK 724), on display in the RAF Museum in England. The Griffon engine replaced the previously used Merlin engine. – Robert Bracken

detect any rivets or seams—a very elegant aircraft.

When 28 Squadron converted to Vampires, the Spit 18s were handed over to a Hong Kong auxiliary squadron—weekend flyers. I don't know if the Mark 24s were brought back to England or not.

Eighty Squadron that was the last squadron on active service to fly the Spitfire—the Mark 24. Called the Bell Squadron, it was named after an outstanding fighter pilot of the First World War. I didn't belong to the squadron itself—I actually belonged to the wing, since I was the weapons officer. However, I did fly in both 28 and 80 Squadron. We also had a Sunderland flying-boat squadron at Hong Kong at that time.

The Spitfire was replaced in RAF service by new jet aircraft. The Vampire and Meteor jets were, in a way, simpler to fly than the Spitfire particularly in landing. The long nose of the Spitfire made it difficult to see the runway on your approach. With the new jets you sat in front of the engine with a great big window. You could see right down the runway and hit it in the first six inches.

Acknowledgments

*This project came to fruition thanks to the advice and participation of a great many people.
I would like to thank as many as I can, as without them, this book would have been impossible.*

Tony Akkerman, artist
Kathy Andrachuck, with thanks for help with Len Thorne, 421 Squadron
Charles Antonio, consultant
Gerry Anglin, writer, war correspondent
Margaret Anglin, history appreciation, advice
Derrick Arnold, aircraft collector, Spitfire pilot
Peter Arnold, Spitfire historian and owner
John and Maureen Atkey, Museum of Flight, Scotland

Thomas Barton
Ronald Bracken, aircraft enthusiast
William and Irene Bracken, my parents, for putting up with my interest in aircraft models and history
Cecil Brown, for great help with proofreading the manuscript
John Burtniak, Brock University Library

Gary Cameron, for help with his dad and information
Olive Carney
Tom Couglin, author of *Dangerous Sky*, for advice
Ralph Clint, aircraft drawings

John DenOuden, Mustang and F-86 pilot and aircraft enthusiast
Betty Doherty, for help with info on 416 Squadron
Irene van Empel, Holland

Bob Finlayson, artist—birds and aircraft

Steven Fochuk

Hugh Godefroy, wing commander
Monica Gomis
George Greenough, ground crew
Stephen Grey, Imperial War Museum Fighter Collection Curator, Duxford

Bill and Dorothy Harper
Bernie Hengst, aircraft historian and model aircraft expert
Walter Henry, Canadian Aviation Historical Society
Ted Hine, Imperial War Museum, London
Dave Hiorth, Canadian Archives
Tom Hitchcock, of Monogram Books, U.S.A.

Ken and Emily James, my employers at James Studio

Johnnie Johnson, A.V.M.
Ken R. Johnson, aviation historian
Michael Johnson, for his hospitality
Christy Johnston, for her interest in "High Flight" by John Magee

Dennis Keegan, Spitfire expert and modeller
Carl Kjarsgaard, aircraft historian
Tim Knutson, aircraft modeller

Bill Lindsay, photographer and artist
Mrs. Lindsay
David Lister, aviation veteran
Ron and Betty Lowry

Duncan MacIntosh
David Magee, brother of John Magee,
    author of "High Flight"
Steve Martin, aviation writer and enthusiast
Dr. Howard McGarry, Mrs. McGarry,
    Rick McGarry
Larry Milberry, aviation writer and historian
Ray and Mary Mills, who run 127 Wing as a
    living tribute to the RCAF and Canadians
    in England

Jennifer Newport
Sue Newman
Ethel Norman, for help regarding her brother
    Robert Zobell

Mrs. Paul Ostrander, for help with Paul's
    logbook and photos
Sylvia and Dick Ostronik, for encouragement
    —the P-38 was a good plane, too
Kim Parnell, BGM Photo Labs

Jeff Robinson, aviation enthusiast and
    modeller
Barbara and Hugh Rooney
Royal Canadian Air Force Association
Peter Rushen, Imperial War Museum, Duxford

Sandy Sanderson, veteran
Steve Sauvé, DND
Shelly Saywell, writer, specializing in
    women's view of the war
Pat and Rosa Simon
Dorothée Skalde
Ray and Ann Steup, aviation enthusiasts
Arthur Steven, artist
Rob Schweyer, archivist for the Canadian
    Warplane Heritage
Don Sutherland, Brock University History
    Professor

George and Kathy Thamas
Dave Thompson, aviation historian
Chris Tothpal, for all her help, especially with
    John Patus
Bernie Traynor, aviation enthusiast

Gord and Mary Underhill

Dwight Whalen, writer
Stan Whiteman
Cliff Whybra, aviation enthusiast and
    modeller
Les Wilkinson, author and Avro Arrow expert
Charles G. Worman, United States Air Force
    Museum
Glen Wright, Canadian Archives

Canadian Fighter Pilots

Thanks to the Canadian Fighter Pilots' Association, and to all those I talked to, including the following:

400 Squadron
Paul Bissky
M.G. Brown
Arthur S. Collins
Laurie Gauld
Ed Maloney,
Ted Walton

401 Squadron
Arthur Bishop
G.D. Cameron
Alvin Harley
I.F. Kennedy
Thomas Koch
Cecil Mann
Don Morrison
Howard C. Nicholson
John Weir

402 Squadron
Bill Austin
Norm Bretz
George Lawson
Brian MacConnell
Robert Morrow
H. Nicholson
Rick Richards
Jack Rigby

403 Squadron
George Aitken
George Beurling (family)
Cec Brown
Norm Chevers
M. Gordon
Charles Magwood
Bob Middlemiss
Noel Ogilvie
Thomas S. Todd
Charles Tomasky
Stu Tosh
Roy Wozniak

411 Squadron
Jack Boyle
Andy McNiece
Chuck Steele
Denny Wilson

412 Squadron
Wilf Banks
Howard Phillips
Bill Roberts

414 Squadron
Arthur Bowman
Ken Lawson

416 Squadron
George Aitken
Chuck Darrow
Dick Forbes-Roberts
Sten Lundberg
John Patus
Art Sager
Walter Thompson
R.H. "Kelly" Walker
F.H. Boulton

417 Squadron
J.J. Doyle
Bert Houle
Cam Everett
Bill Whitside

421 Squadron
Alan Bayly
Richard "Hap" Beall
Phil Blades
Danny Browne
Lloyd Burford
D. Carlson (Padre)
Wally Conrad
Ron Gillies
Fred Green
Mac Gordon
Lloyd Hennessy
Bill Marshall
Ron McGarva
"Tank" McIntosh
Les McKellar
John Sherlock

430 Squadron
Bill Golden
W. Middleton
Richard Rohmer

441 Squadron
Sid Bregman
Ron Lake
Guy Mott
Bill Reale
Hughie Ritchie
R.H. "Kelly" Walker

The Spitfire V, AE-H (AB 910), restored in 1994 to its original D-Day colours based on research by the author. This aircraft is still flown by the RAF. – Robert Bracken

442 Squadron
Al Bathurst
William Weeks

443 Squadron
Ed Ferguson
Les Foster
George Greenough
Lloyd Hunt
Gord Ockenden
Art Sager (S/L)
Ivor Williams

ATA
Marian Orr
Violet Warren

RCAF Rockliffe
Chuck Doodson
Tom Percival

RAF
155 Squadron
Paul Ostrander

609 Squadron
Keith Ogilvie
Jan Zurakowski

234 Squadron
J.S. Young

185 Squadron
Noel Ogilvie

541, 543 PR
Tet Walston

VICKERS-SUPERMARINE TYPE 331 SPITFIRE F VB Drawn by: A.R. Clint Date: 9/94

see scale below

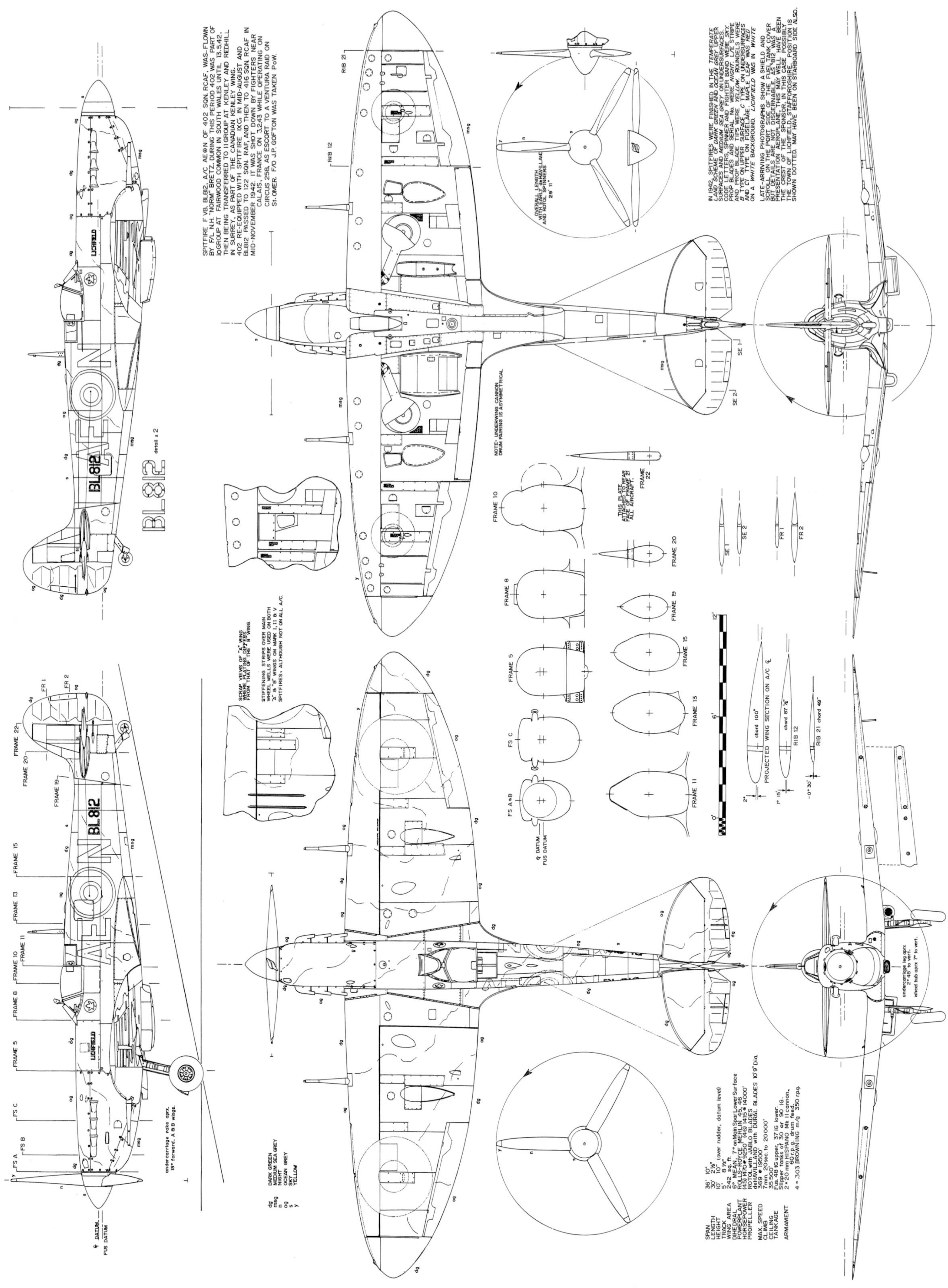

VICKERS-SUPERMARINE TYPE 361 SPITFIRE F IX C

Drawn by: A.R. Clint Date: 10/94

see scale below

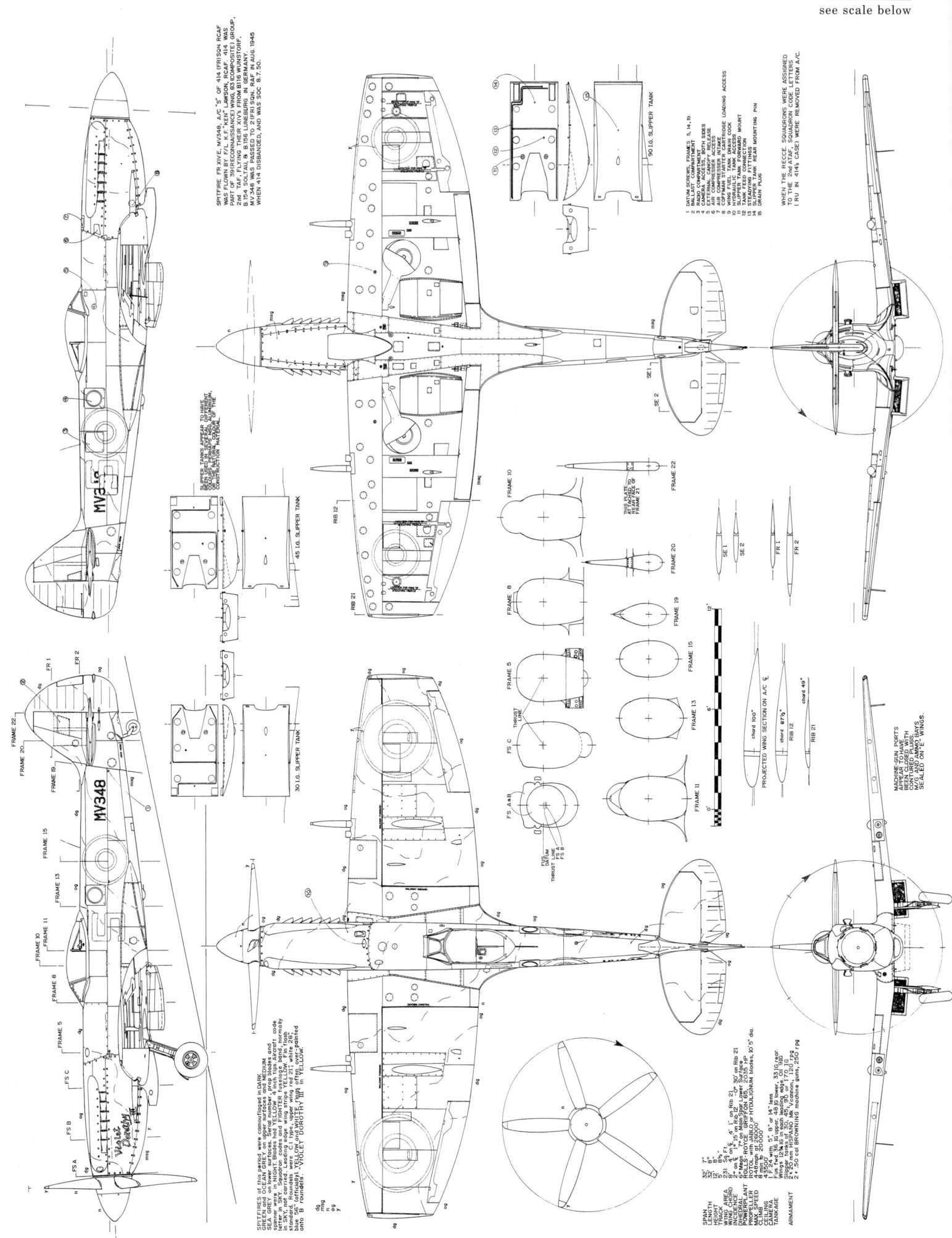

VICKERS-SUPERMARINE TYPE 379   SPITFIRE FR XIV E   Drawn by: A.R. Clint   Date: 11/94

see scale below

VICKERS-SUPERMARINE TYPE 361   SPITFIRE LF XVI E   Drawn by: A.R. Clint   Date: 11/94

see scale below

VICKERS-SUPERMARINE SPITFIRES

Drawn by: A.R. Clint   Date: 2/95

see scale below

DRAWN BY: A.R. CLINT | SCALE 1:24 | REPRO 1:72 | DATE FEB 95

V-S TYPE 329 SPITFIRE F IIA — P7679

V-S TYPE 352 SPITFIRE F VB (tropicalized) — ER640

V-S TYPE 360 SPITFIRE F VIII — JF627

V-S TYPE 361 SPITFIRE F IXC — BR138

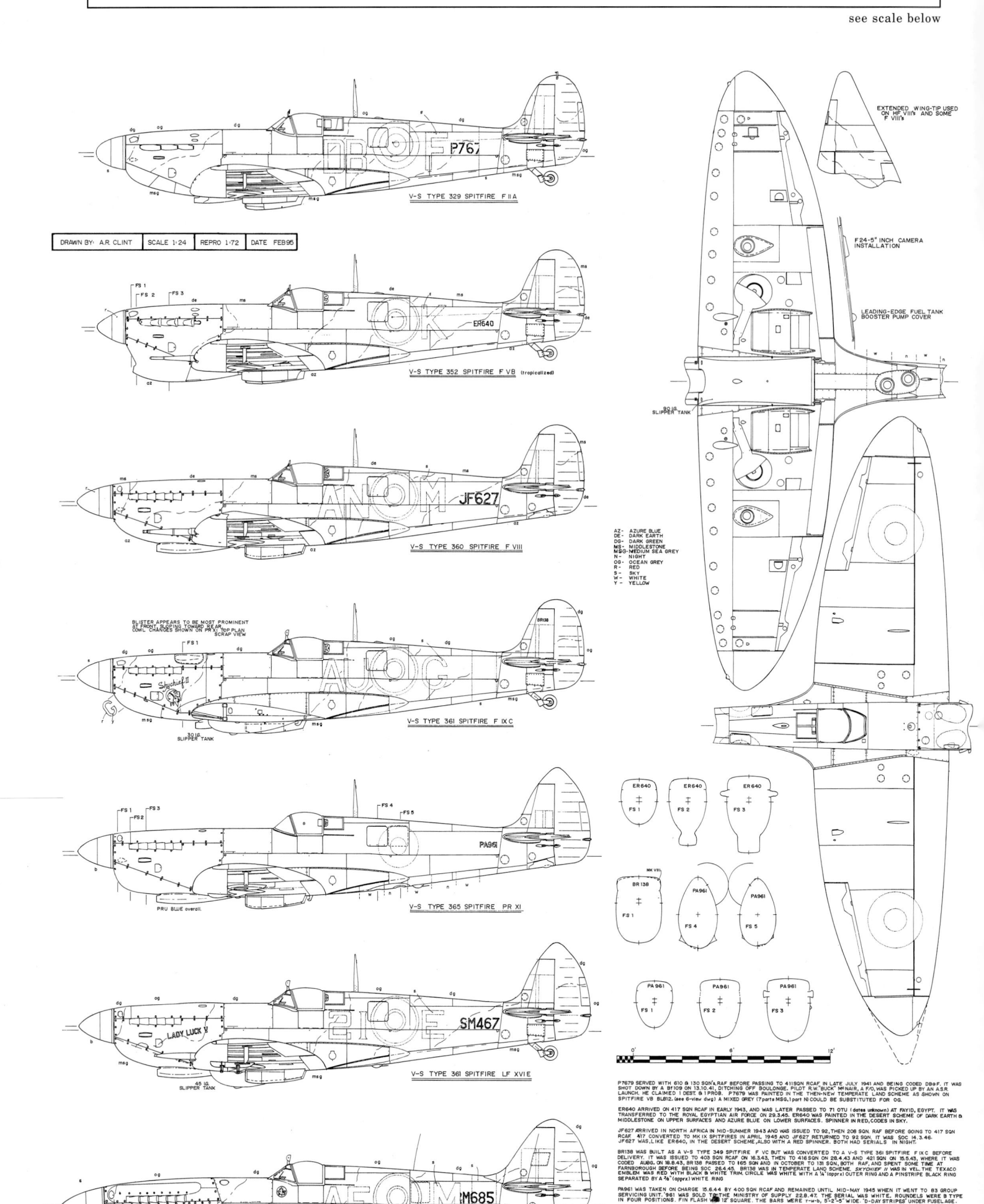

V-S TYPE 365 SPITFIRE PR XI — PA961 (PRU BLUE overall)

V-S TYPE 361 SPITFIRE LF XVI E — SM467 (LADY LUCK V)

V-S TYPE 379 SPITFIRE F XIVE — RM685

EXTENDED WING-TIP USED ON HF VIII'S AND SOME F VIII's

F 24-5" INCH CAMERA INSTALLATION

LEADING-EDGE FUEL TANK BOOSTER PUMP COVER

SLIPPER TANK

Colour key:
- AZ — AZURE BLUE
- DE — DARK EARTH
- DG — DARK GREEN
- MS — MIDDLESTONE
- MSG — MEDIUM SEA GREY
- N — NIGHT
- OG — OCEAN GREY
- R — RED
- S — SKY
- W — WHITE
- Y — YELLOW

BLISTER APPEARS TO BE MOST PROMINENT AT FRONT, SLOPING TOWARD REAR. COWL CHANGES SHOWN ON PR XI TOP PLAN SCRAP VIEW

45 I.G. SLIPPER TANK

P7679 SERVED WITH 610 & 130 SQN's RAF BEFORE PASSING TO 411 SQN RCAF IN LATE JULY 1941 AND BEING CODED DB⚬F. IT WAS SHOT DOWN BY A Bf 109 ON 13.10.41, DITCHING OFF BOULOGNE. PILOT R.W. "BUCK" McNAIR, A F/O, WAS PICKED UP BY AN A.S.R. LAUNCH. HE CLAIMED 1 DEST. & 1 PROB. P7679 WAS PAINTED IN THE THEN-NEW TEMPERATE LAND SCHEME AS SHOWN ON SPITFIRE VB BL812. (see 6-view dwg) A MIXED GREY (7 parts MSG, 1 part N) COULD BE SUBSTITUTED FOR OG.

ER640 ARRIVED ON 417 SQN RCAF IN EARLY 1943, AND WAS LATER PASSED TO 71 OTU (dates unknown) AT FAYID, EGYPT. IT WAS TRANSFERRED TO THE ROYAL EGYPTIAN AIR FORCE ON 29.3.45. ER640 WAS PAINTED IN THE DESERT SCHEME OF DARK EARTH & MIDDLESTONE ON UPPER SURFACES AND AZURE BLUE ON LOWER SURFACES. SPINNER IN RED, CODES IN SKY.

JF627 ARRIVED IN NORTH AFRICA IN MID-SUMMER 1943 AND WAS ISSUED TO 92, THEN 208 SQN. RAF BEFORE GOING TO 417 SQN RCAF. 417 CONVERTED TO MK IX SPITFIRES IN APRIL 1945 AND JF627 RETURNED TO 92 SQN. IT WAS SOC 14.3.46. JF627 WAS, LIKE ER640, IN THE DESERT SCHEME, ALSO WITH A RED SPINNER. BOTH HAD SERIALS IN NIGHT.

BR138 WAS BUILT AS A V-S TYPE 349 SPITFIRE F VC BUT WAS CONVERTED TO A V-S TYPE 361 SPITFIRE F IXC BEFORE DELIVERY. IT WAS ISSUED TO 403 SQN RCAF ON 16.3.43, THEN TO 416 SQN ON 28.4.43 AND 421 SQN ON 15.5.43, WHERE IT WAS CODED AU⚬G. ON 18.8.43, BR138 PASSED TO 165 SQN AND IN OCTOBER TO 131 SQN, BOTH RAF, AND SPENT SOME TIME AT FARNBOROUGH BEFORE BEING SOC 26.4.45. BR138 WAS IN TEMPERATE LAND SCHEME. SKYCHIEF II WAS IN YEL. THE TEXACO EMBLEM WAS RED WITH BLACK & WHITE TRIM. CIRCLE WAS WHITE WITH A ¼" (apprx) OUTER RING AND A PINSTRIPE BLACK RING SEPARATED BY A ⅜" (apprx) WHITE RING.

PA961 WAS TAKEN ON CHARGE 15.6.44 BY 400 SQN RCAF AND REMAINED UNTIL MID-MAY 1945 WHEN IT WENT TO 83 GROUP SERVICING UNIT. '961 WAS SOLD TO THE MINISTRY OF SUPPLY 22.8.47. THE SERIAL WAS WHITE. ROUNDELS WERE B TYPE IN FOUR POSITIONS. FIN FLASH WAS 12" SQUARE. THE BARS WERE r-w-b, 5'-2"-5" WIDE. "D-DAY STRIPES" UNDER FUSELAGE.

SM467 WAS DELIVERED TO 443 SQN RCAF ON 1.2.45 AND BECAME THE PRIMARY MOUNT OF F/L L.E. HUNT. AFTER A FLYING ACCIDENT IN LATE MARCH '467 WAS TURNED OVER TO 410 REPAIR & SALVAGE UNIT. IT WAS SOC 7.3.46. SM467, LADY LUCK V (white) WAS PAINTED IN THE SAME SCHEME AS SPITFIRE LF XVI E TB886 (see 6-view dwg).

RM685 WAS ALLOTTED TO 402 SQN IN MID-JULY 1944 AND WAS FLOWN UNTIL 23.8.44 WHEN IT WAS INVOLVED IN A FLYING ACCIDENT AND LEFT THE SQN. AFTER REPAIRS IT WAS STORED UNTIL SOLD TO THE BELGIAN AIR FORCE 25.7.47, RECEIVING SERIAL SG 15. RM685 WAS IN TEMPERATE LAND SCHEME. A RED MAPLE LEAF ON A WHITE BACKGROUND WAS ON THE FUEL TANK COVER SIDES. NOTE CENTRE INVASION STRIPE CARRIED FORWARD ON FILLET TOP SURFACE.